The Complete Poems

BASIL BUNTING

The Complete Poems

ASSOCIATE EDITOR
RICHARD CADDEL

Oxford   New York
OXFORD UNIVERSITY PRESS

Oxford University Press, Walton Street, Oxford OX2 6DP

Oxford New York

Athens Auckland Bangkok Bogota Bombay
Buenos Aires Calcutta Cape Town Dar es Salaam
Delhi Florence Hong Kong Istanbul Karachi
Kuala Lumpur Madras Madrid Melbourne
Mexico City Nairobi Paris Singapore
Taipei Tokyo Toronto

and associated companies in
Berlin Ibadan

Oxford is a trade mark of Oxford University Press

First published in Oxford Poets
as an Oxford University Press paperback 1994
Reissued 1996

British Library Cataloguing in Publication Data
Data available

Library of Congress Cataloging in Publication Data
Bunting, Basil.
[Poems]
The complete poems / Basil Bunting; associate editor, Richard
Caddel.
p.   cm.—(Oxford poets)
Includes index.
I. Caddel, Richard, 1949–   .   II. Title.   III. Series.
PR6003.U36A17 1994   821'.914—dc20   93–48950
ISBN 0–19–282282–9

3 5 7 9 10 8 6 4

Printed in Hong Kong

ACKNOWLEDGEMENTS

For permissions to reproduce poems and other material from archives and special collections: to the Basil Bunting Poetry Archive, University Library, University of Durham, for 'Such syllables flicker out of grass', 'Hi, tent-boy, get that tent down', 'You've come! O how flustered and anxious . . .', 'Ginger, who are you going with?', 'That filly couldnt carry a rider', 'Snow's on the fellside, look!', and *The Pious Cat*; to the Collection of American Literature, Beinecke Rare Book and Manuscript Library, Yale University, for poems from *Caveat Emptor*, the Bartok limerick and Bunting's comment on it; to the Harry Ransom Humanities Research Center, University of Texas at Austin, for 'Envoi to the Reader', 'Amru'l Qais and Labīd and Akhtal', 'Noah's son' and Bunting's comment on that piece; to the Poetry/Rare Books Collection, University Libraries, University at Buffalo, Buffalo, NY, for 'A Song for Rustam' and 'To abate what swells'.

To the Headmasters of Ackworth and Leighton Park Schools, for the use of Bunting's school poems and permission to reprint material from their school archives and magazines.

CONTENTS

SECOND BOOK OF ODES

OVERDRAFTS

ix

NOTES

APPENDICES   217

INDEX OF TITLES AND FIRST LINES   223

A NOTE ON THE TEXT

Bunting's poems accumulated slowly. His first substantial collection came when he was fifty, with the publication of *Poems: 1950* (Cleaner's Press, Galveston). Here we find for the first time the basic arrangement (Sonatas: Odes: Overdrafts), and to a great extent the sequence of poems which was to be worked on and added to over the next thirty-five years. *Loquitur* (1965), published by Stuart Montgomery's Fulcrum Press, extended the range and tinkered the sequence towards its final form. At the same time came *The Spoils* (Morden Tower Bookroom, 1965) and *Briggflatts* (Fulcrum, 1966). These elements, together with the Second Book of Odes, were gathered together in Fulcrum's *Collected Poems* (1968), the collection which established Bunting's reputation in Britain and America. This edition was reproduced, with some extra poems and corrections, by Oxford University Press (1978). A final ode was added to an American edition (Moyer Bell, Mt. Kisco, 1985) nine days before his death.

This edition presents a complete corrected resetting of the final text of Bunting's *Collected Poems* as it stood at his death in 1985. That is the heart of the book. To that is added work which remained uncollected at that time: the long poem–translation for children which Bunting had sought to publish separately in his lifetime; other poems and translations which had fallen by the wayside, and in appendices all that he published in the way of juvenilia, and two limericks. Much of this supplementary work was gathered in *Uncollected Poems* (Oxford University Press, 1991). This edition thus brings all Bunting's published poetry together in a single volume for the first time.

The title is perhaps misleading: an academically complete edition, which would contain all Bunting's fragments and variants, letter–poems, and poems of dubious ascription, must await another editor in an age when all the manuscript and typescript remains of Bunting have been docketed and indexed. As partial repayment of my own debt to Bunting, my task has been to shape a book which is complete for readers of poetry.

I am grateful for the continued support and encouragement of Bunting's family, Sima Bunting, Tom and Maria Bunting, and John Halliday. I also acknowledge my debt to colleagues and supporters of the Basil Bunting Poetry Centre at Durham University; and to individuals such as Harry Gilonis, Peter

Makin and Peter Quartermain, for their comments and advice, and to my family, for their support and patience. Errors and oversights remain my own.

Richard Caddel
Durham, August 1993

COLLECTED POEMS

PREFACE

A man who collects his poems screws together the boards of his coffin. Those outside will have all the fun, but he is entitled to his last confession. These verses were written here and there now and then over forty years and four continents. Heaped together they make a book.

If ever I learned the trick of it, it was mostly from poets long dead whose names are obvious: Wordsworth and Dante, Horace, Wyat and Malherbe, Manuchehri and Ferdosi, Villon, Whitman, Edmund Spenser; but two living men also taught me much: Ezra Pound and in his sterner, stonier way, Louis Zukofsky. It would not be fitting to collect my poems without mentioning them.

With sleights learned from others and an ear open to melodic analogies I have set down words as a musician pricks his score, not to be read in silence, but to trace in the air a pattern of sound that may sometimes, I hope, be pleasing. Unabashèd boys and girls may enjoy them. This book is theirs.

I am grateful to those who printed my poems from time to time, above all to *Poetry*, of Chicago, whose editors have been kind to me one after another.

Basil Bunting
1968

A new edition of this book has given me a chance to put right a few words and stops the compositor got wrong, and to add four short new poems. A fifth seemed better lost.

1977

There is one solitary short poem that I have added to the collected volume.

1985

SONATAS

VILLON

I

He whom we anatomized
'whose words we gathered as pleasant flowers
and thought on his wit and how neatly he described things'
speaks
to us, hatching marrow,
broody all night over the bones of a deadman.

My tongue is a curve in the ear. Vision is lies.
We saw it so and it was not so,
the Emperor with the Golden Hands, the Virgin in blue.
(—A blazing parchment,
Matthew Paris his kings in blue and gold.)

It was not so,
scratched on black by God knows who,
by God, by God knows who.

In the dark in fetters
on bended elbows I supported my weak back
hulloing to muffled walls blank again
unresonant. It was gone, is silent, is always silent.
My soundbox lacks sonority. All but inaudible
I stammer to my ear:
Naked speech! Naked beggar both blind and cold!
Wrap it for my sake in Paisley shawls and bright soft fabric,
wrap it in curves and cover it with sleek lank hair.

What trumpets? What bright hands? Fetters, it was the Emperor
with magic in darkness, I unforewarned.
The golden hands are not in Averrhoes,
eyes lie and this swine's fare bread and water
makes my head wuzz. Have pity, have pity on me!

To the right was darkness and to the left hardness
below hardness darkness above
at the feet darkness at the head partial hardness

with equal intervals without
to the left moaning and beyond a scurry.
In those days rode the good Lorraine
whom English burned at Rouen,
the day's bones whitening in centuries' dust.

Then he saw his ghosts glitter with golden hands,
the Emperor sliding up and up from his tomb
alongside Charles. These things are not obliterate.
White gobs spitten for mockery;
and I too shall have CY GIST written over me.

Remember, imbeciles and wits,
sots and ascetics, fair and foul,
young girls with little tender tits,
that DEATH is written over all.

Worn hides that scarcely clothe the soul
they are so rotten, old and thin,
or firm and soft and warm and full—
fellmonger Death gets every skin.

All that is piteous, all that's fair,
all that is fat and scant of breath,
Elisha's baldness, Helen's hair,
is Death's collateral:

Three score and ten years after sight
of this pay me your pulse and breath
value received. And who dare cite,
as we forgive our debtors, Death?

Abelard and Eloise,
Henry the Fowler, Charlemagne,
Genée, Lopokova, all these
die, die in pain.

And General Grant and General Lee,
Patti and Florence Nightingale,
like Tyro and Antiope
drift among ghosts in Hell,

know nothing, are nothing, save a fume
driving across a mind
preoccupied with this: our doom
is, to be sifted by the wind,

heaped up, smoothed down like silly sands.
We are less permanent than thought.
The Emperor with the Golden Hands

is still a word, a tint, a tone,
insubstantial-glorious,
when we ourselves are dead and gone
and the green grass growing over us.

II

Let his days be few and let
his bishoprick pass to another,
for he fed me on carrion and on a dry crust,
mouldy bread that his dogs had vomited,
I lying on my back in the dark place, in the grave,
fettered to a post in the damp cellarage.
      Whereinall we differ not. But they have swept the floor,
there are no dancers, no somersaulters now,
only bricks and bleak black cement and bricks,
only the military tread and the snap of the locks.
      Mine was a threeplank bed whereon
I lay and cursed the weary sun.
They took away the prison clothes
and on the frosty nights I froze.
I had a Bible where I read
that Jesus came to raise the dead—
I kept myself from going mad
by singing an old bawdy ballad
and birds sang on my windowsill
and tortured me till I was ill,
but Archipiada came to me
and comforted my cold body
and Circe excellent utterer of her mind
lay with me in that dungeon for a year

making a silk purse from an old sow's ear
till Ronsard put a thimble on her tongue.

　　　Whereinall we differ not. But they have named all the stars,
trodden down the scrub of the desert, run the white moon to a
　　　　　　　　　　　　　　　　　　　　　　　　schedule,
Joshua's serf whose beauty drove men mad.
They have melted the snows from Erebus, weighed the clouds,
hunted down the white bear, hunted the whale the seal the
　　　　　　　　　　　　　　　　　　　　　　　kangaroo,
they have set private enquiry agents onto Archipiada:
What is your name? Your maiden name?
Go in there to be searched. I suspect it is not your true name.
Distinguishing marks if any? (O anthropometrics!)
Now the thumbprints for filing.
Colour of hair? of eyes? of hands? O Bertillon!
How many golden prints on the smudgy page?
Homer? Adest. Dante? Adest.
Adsunt omnes, omnes et
Villon.
Villon?
Blacked by the sun, washed by the rain,
hither and thither scurrying as the wind varies.

　　　　　　　III

　　　　　　Under the olive trees
　　　　　　walking alone
　　　　　　on the green terraces
　　　　　　very seldom
　　　　　　over the sea seldom
　　　　　　where it ravelled and spun
　　　　　　blue tapestries white and green
　　　　　　gravecloths of men
　　　　　　Romans and modern men
　　　　　　and the men of the sea
　　　　　　who have neither nation nor time
　　　　　　on the mountains seldom
　　　　　　the white mountains beyond
　　　　　　or the brown mountains between
　　　　　　and their drifting echoes

in the clouds and over the sea
in shrines on their ridges
the goddess of the country
silverplated in silk and embroidery
with offerings of pictures
little ships and arms
below me the ports
with naked breasts
shipless spoiled sacked
because of the beauty of Helen

precision clarifying vagueness;
boundary to a wilderness
of detail; chisel voice
smoothing the flanks of noise;
catalytic making whisper and whisper
run together like two drops of quicksilver;
factor that resolves
        unnoted harmonies;
name of the nameless;
        stuff that clings
to frigid limbs
        more marble hard
than girls imagined by Mantegna . . .

The sea has no renewal, no forgetting,
no variety of death,
is silent with the silence of a single note.

How can I sing with my love in my bosom?
Unclean, immature and unseasonable salmon.

1925

ATTIS: OR, SOMETHING MISSING

SONATINA

> *Dea magna, dea Cybele, dea domina Dindymi,*
> *procul a mea tuus sit furor omnis, era, domo:*
> *alios age incitatos, alios age rabidos.*

I

Out of puff
noonhot in tweeds and gray felt,
tired of appearance and
disappearance;
warm obese frame limp with satiety;
slavishly circumspect at sixty;
he spreads over the ottoman
scanning the pictures and table trinkets.

(That hand's dismissed shadow
moves through fastidiously selective consciousness,
rearranges pain.)

There are no colours, words only,
and measured shaking of strings,
and flutes and oboes
enough for dancers.
. . . .   reluctant ebb:
        salt from all beaches:
disrupt Atlantis, days forgotten,
extinct peoples, silted harbours.
He regrets that brackish
        train of the huntress
driven into slackening fresh,
expelled when the
        estuary resumes
colourless potability;
        wreckage that drifted
in drifts out.

12

'Longranked larches succeed larches, spokes of a
stroll; hounds trooping around hooves; and the stolid horn's
sweet breath. *Voice:* Have you seen the
fox? Which way did he go, he go?
There was soft rain.
I recollect deep mud and leafmould somewhere: and
in the distance Cheviot's
heatherbrown flanks and white cap.

Landscape salvaged from
evinced notice of
superabundance, of
since parsimonious
soil . . . . .
         Mother of Gods.'

Mother of eunuchs.

Praise the green earth. Chance has appointed her
      home, workshop, larder, middenpit.
      Her lousy skin scabbed here and there by
      cities provides us with name and nation.

From her brooks sweat. Hers corn and fruit.
      Earthquakes are hers too. Ravenous animals
      are sent by her. Praise her and call her
      Mother and Mother of Gods and Eunuchs.

II

(*Variations on a theme by Milton*)

I thought I saw my late wife (a very respectable woman)
coming from Bywell churchyard with a handful of raisins.
I was not pleased, it is shocking to meet a ghost, so I cut her
and went and sat amongst the rank watergrasses by the Tyne.

Centrifugal tutus! Sarabands!
music clear enough to
pluck stately dances from

13

madness before the frenzy.
Andante . . . . *Prestissimo!*
turbulent my Orfeo!
A tumult softly hissed
as by muted violins,
Tesiphone's, Alecto's
capillary orchestra.
Long phrases falling like
intermittent private voices
suddenly in the midst of talk,
falling aslant like last light:
VENGA MEDUSA
VENGA
MEDUSA SÌ L'FAREM DI SMALTO
Send for Medusa: we'll enamel him!

Long loved and
too long loved, stale habit, such decay of ardour,
love never dead, love never hoping, never gay.
Ageslow venom selfsecreted. Such shame!

The gorgon's method:
    In the morning
clean streets welcomed light's renewal,
patient, passive to the weight of buses
thundering like cabinet ministers
over a lethargic populace.
Streets buffeted thin soles at midday,
streets full of beggars.
Battered, filthily unfortunate streets
perish, their ghosts are wretched
in the mockery of lamps.

And O Purveyor
of geraniums and pianos to the Kaiserin!
the hot smell of the street
conversing with the bleat
of rancid air streaming up tenement stairways!

Gods awake and fierce
stalk across the night
grasping favour of men,

power to hurt or endow,
      leave to inhabit
figure and name; or skulk
from impotence in light's
      opacity.
Day hides them, opaque day
hides their promenades; night
reveals them stalking
      (VENGA MEDUSA)
      passionately.

Polymnia
keeps a cafe in Reno.
Well, (eh, Cino?)
I dare no longer raise my eyes
on any lass
seeing what one of them has done to me.
So singlehearted, so steady
never lover, none so humble.
She made a new youth lord of her.
I lower my eyes. I say:
'I will not look on any,
maybe all are jilts.'

III

Pastorale arioso
(falsetto)

What mournful stave, what bellow shakes the grove?
O, it is Attis grieving for his testicles!
Attis stiffening amid the snows
and the wind whining through his hair and fingers!

'Pines, my sisters, I, your sister,
chaffered for lambs in the marketplace.
I also won the 14 carat halfhunter goldwatch
at the annual sports and flowershow.
The young girls simpered when I passed.
Now I am out of a job. I would like to be lady's-maid
      to Dindyma.

15

Pines, my sisters, I, your sister,
tended the bull and the entire horse.
Pensive geldings gape stale adolescence religiously,
yearning for procreative energy;
call it God. I sat amongst the atheists,
I was bankrupted by affiliation orders
who now bow my chaste vegetable forehead
            to Dindyma.

Pines, my sisters, I, your sister,
parch in calm weather, swelter in Scirocco, sway in northwind,
I am passive to the heave of spring.
In the season I will pay my phallic harvest
            to Dindyma.

Dindyma! Dindyma!
The wraith of my manhood,
the cruel ghost of my manhood,
            limp in hell,
leapt sleeplessly in strange beds.
I have forgotten most of the details,
            most of the names,
            and the responses to
            the ithyphallic hymns:
            forgotten the syntax,
            and the paradigms
grate scrappily against reluctant nerves.

(Oh Sis!
I've been 'ad!
I've been 'ad proper!)

Shall we be whole in Elysium?
I am rooted in you,
            Dindyma!
      assure me
      the roses and myrtles,
      the lavish roses,
      the naively
      portentous myrtles,
corroborate the peacock.

(I've been 'ad!)'

To whom Cybele:
          'The peacock's knavery
          keeps you in slavery.
          The roses cheat
          you, butcher's meat.
          The myrtles' pretence
          offends commonsense.
          Yet a muse defrauds
          the Mother of the Gods.
          Ponder this allegorical
          oracle.'

                              Attis his embleme:
                              Nonnulla deest.

                                        1931

AUS DEM ZWEITEN REICH

I

Women swarm in Tauentsienstrasse.
Clients of Nollendorferplatz cafés,
shadows on sweaty glass,
hum, drum on the table
           to the negerband's faint jazz.
Humdrum at the table.

Hour and hour
meeting against me,
efficiently whipped cream,
efficiently metropolitan chatter and snap,
transparent glistening wrapper
           for a candy pack.

Automatic, somewhat too clean,
body and soul similarly scented,
on time,
rapid, dogmatic, automatic and efficient,
ganz modern.

'Sturm über Asien' is off, some other flicker . . .
Kiss me in the taxi, twist fingers in the dark.
A box of chocolates is necessary.
I am preoccupied with Sie and Du.
           The person on the screen,
divorced and twenty-five, must pass for fourteen
for the story's sake, an insipidity
contrived to dress her in shorts
and a widenecked shirt with nothing underneath
so that you see her small breasts when she
often bends towards the camera.
Audience mainly male stirs,
           I am teased too,
I like this public blonde better than my brunette,
           but that will never do.
—Let's go,

arm in arm on foot over gleaming snow
past the Gedächtnis Kirche
to the loud crowded cafés near the Bahnhof Zoo.

Better hugged together ('to keep warm')
under street trees whimpering to the keen wind
over snow whispering to many feet,
find out a consolingly mediocre
neighbourhood without music, varnished faces
bright and sagacious against varnished walls,
youngsters red from skating,
businessmen reading the papers:
no need to talk—much:
what indolence supplies.
'If, smoothing this silk skirt, you pinch my thighs,
that will be fabelhaft.'

II

Herr Lignitz knows Old Berlin. It is near the Post Office
with several rather disorderly public houses.
'You have no naked pictures in your English magazines.
It is shocking. Berlin is very shocking to the English. Are you
                                        shocked?
Would you like to see the naked cabarets
in Jaegerstrasse? I think there is
nothing like that in Paris.
Or a department store? They are said to be
almost equal to Macy's in America.'

III

The renowned author of
more plays than Shakespeare
stopped and did his hair
with a pocket glass
before entering the village,
afraid they wouldnt recognize

caricature and picturepostcard,
that windswept chevelure.

Who talked about poetry,
and he said nothing at all;
plays,
and he said nothing at all;
politics,
and he stirred as if a flea
bit him
but wouldnt let on in company;
and the frost in Berlin,
muttered: 𝕾𝖈𝖍𝖗𝖊𝖈𝖐𝖑𝖎𝖈𝖍

Viennese bow from the hips,
notorieties
contorted laudatory lips,
wreaths and bouquets surround
the mindless menopause.
Stillborn fecundities,
frostbound applause.

1931

THE WELL OF LYCOPOLIS

cujus potu signa
virginitatis eripiuntur

I

Advis m'est que j'oy regretter

Slinking by the jug-and-bottle
swingdoor I fell in with
Mother Venus, ageing, bedraggled, a
half-quartern of gin under her shawl,
wishing she was a young girl again:
'It's cruel hard to be getting old so soon.
I wonder I dont kill myself and have done with it.

I had them all on a string at one time,
lawyers, doctors, business-men:
there wasnt a man alive but would have given
all he possessed
for what they wont take now free for nothing.
I turned them down,
I must have had no sense,
for the sake of a shifty young fellow:
whatever I may have done at other times
on the sly
I was in love then and no mistake;
and him always knocking me about
and only cared for my money.
However much he shook me or kicked me I
loved him just the same.
If he'd made me take in washing he'd
only have had to say: 'Give us a kiss'
and I'd have forgotten my troubles.
The selfish pig, never up to any good!
He used to cuddle me. Fat lot of good it's done me!
What did I get out of it besides a bad conscience?

But he's been dead longer than thirty years
and I'm still here, old and skinny.
When I think about the old days,
what I was like and what I'm like now,
it fair drives me crazy to
look at myself with nothing on.
What a change!
Miserable dried up skin and bone.

But none of their Bacchic impertinence,
medicinal stout nor portwine-cum-beef.
A dram of anaesthetic, brother.
I'm a British subject if I *am* a colonial,
distilled liquor's clean.
It's the times have changed. I remember during the War
kids carrying the clap to school under their pinnies,
studying Belgian atrocities in the Sunday papers
or the men pissing in the backstreets; and grown women
sweating their shifts sticky at the smell of khaki
every little while.
Love's an encumberance to them who
rinse carefully before using, better
keep yourself to yourself.
What it is to be in the movement!
'Follow the instructions on page fortyone'
unlovely labour of love,
'or work it off in a day's walk,
a cold douche and brisk rub down,
there's nothing like it.'
Aye, tether me among the maniacs,
it's nicer to rave than reason.'

Took her round to Polymnia's, Polymnia
glowering stedfastly at the lukewarm
undusted grate grim with cinders
never properly kindled, the brass head of the
tongs creaking as she twitched them:
'Time is, was, has been.'
A gassy fizzling spun from among the cinders.
The air, an emulsion of some unnameable oil,
greased our napes. We rhymed our breath
to the mumble of coke distilling.

'What have you come for? Why have you brought the
                              Goddess? You who
finger the goods you cannot purchase,
snuffle the skirt you dare not clutch.
There was never love between us, never less
than when you reckoned much. A tool
not worth the negligible price. A fool
not to be esteemed for barren honesty.
Leave me alone. A long time ago
there were men in the world, dances, guitars, ah!
Tell me, Love's mother, have I wrinkles? grey hair?
teats, or dugs? calves, or shanks?
Do I wear unbecoming garments?'

'Blotched belly, slack buttock and breast,
there's little to strip for now.
A few years makes a lot of difference.
Would you have known me?
Poor old fools,
gabbing about our young days,
squatted round a bit of fire
just lit and flickering out already:
and we used to be so pretty!'

II

May my libation of flat beer stood overnight
sour on your stomach, my devoutly worshipped ladies,
may you retch cold bile.
Windy water slurred the glint of Canopus,
am I answerable? Left, the vane
screwing perpetually ungainlywards.
What reply will a
June hailstorm countenance?

'Let's be cosy,
sit it out hand in hand.
Dreaming of you, that's all I do.'
Eiderdown air, any
girl or none, it's the same thing,

23

coats the tongue the morning after.
Answer?
If words were stone, if the sun's lilt
could be fixed in the stone's convexity.
Open your eyes, Polymnia,
at the sleek, slick lads treading gingerly between the bedpots,
stripped buff-naked all but their hats to raise,
and nothing rises but the hats;
smooth, with soft steps, *ambiguoque voltu.*

Daphnis investigated
bubless Chloe
behind a boulder.
Still, they say,
in another climate
virgin with virgin
coupled taste
wine without headache
and the songs are simple.
We have laid on Lycopolis water.
The nights are not fresh
between High Holborn and the Euston Road,
nor the days bright even in summer
nor the grass of the squares green.

Neither (*aequora pontis*)
on the sea's bulge
would the 'proud, full sail'
avail
us, stubborn against the trades,
closehauled,
stiff, flat canvas;
our fingers bleed
under the nail
when we reef.

III

Infamous poetry, abject love,
Aeolus' hand under her frock
this morning. This afternoon
Ocean licking her privities.
Every thrust of the autumn sun
cuckolding
in the green grin of late-flowering trees.
I shall never have anything to myself

but stare in the tank, see
Hell's constellations,
a dogstar for the Dogstar:
women's faces
blank or trivial,
still or rippled water,
a fool's image.

At my time of life it is easier not to see,
much easier to tra-la-la
a widowed tune in poor circumstances—
                    tweet, tweet, twaddle,
                    tweet, tweet, twat.
Squalid acquiescence in the cast-offs
of reputed poetry. Here, Bellerophon,
is a livery hack, a gelding,
easy pace, easy to hire,
all mansuetude and indifference.

Abject poetry, infamous love,
howling like a damp dog in November.
Scamped spring, squandered summer,
grain, husk, stem and stubble
mildewed; mawkish dough and sour bread.
                    Tweet, tweet, twaddle. Endure
detail by detail the cunnilingual law.
'Clap a clout on your jowl for
Jesus sake! Fy for shame!
After hours, is it? or under age?
Hack off his pendants!
Can a moment of madness make up for
an age of consent?'

—with their snouts in the trough,
kecking at gummy guts,
slobbering offal, gobbling potato parings,
yellow cabbage leaves, choking on onion skin,
herring bones, slops of porridge.
Way-O! Bully boys blow!
The Gadarene swihine have got us in tow.

IV

Ed anche vo' che tu per certo credi
che sotto l'acqua ha gente che sospira.

Stuck in the mud they are saying: 'We were sad
in the air, the sweet air the sun makes merry,
we were glum of ourselves, without a reason;
now we are stuck in the mud and therefore sad.'
That's what they mean, but the words die in their throat;
they cannot speak out because they are stuck in the mud.
Stuck, stick, Styx. Styx, eternal, a dwelling.
But the rivers of Paradise,
the sweep of the mountains they rise in?
Drunk or daft hear
a chuckle of spring water:
drowsy suddenly wake,
but the bright peaks have faded.
Who had love for love
whose love was strong or fastidious?
Shadow and shadow noon shrinks, night shelters,
the college of Muses reconstructs
in flimsy drizzle of starlight:
bandy, hunchback, dot-and-carry-one,
praised-for-a-guinea.

Join the Royal Air Force
and See the World. The Navy will
Make a Man of You. Tour India with the Flag.
One of the ragtime army,
involuntary volunteer,
queued up for the pox in Rouen. What a blighty!

Surrendered in March. Or maybe
ulcers of mustard gas, a rivet in the lung
from scrappy shrapnel,
frostbite, trench-fever, shell-shock,
self-inflicted wound,
tetanus, malaria, influenza.
Swapped your spare boots for a packet of gaspers.
Overstayed leave.
Debauched the neighbor's little girl
to save two shillings . . .

muttering inaudibly beneath the quagmire,
irresolute, barren, dependent, this page
ripped from Love's ledger and Poetry's:
and besides I want you to know for certain
there are people under the water. They are sighing.
The surface bubbles and boils with their sighs.
Look where you will you see it.
The surface sparkles and dances with their sighs
as though Styx were silvered by a wind from Heaven.

1935

THE SPOILS   الإنفال لله

*These are the sons of Shem, after
their families, after their tongues,
in their lands, after their nations.*

Man's life so little worth,
do we fear to take or lose it?
No ill companion on a journey, Death
lays his purse on the table and opens the wine.

ASSHUR:
As I sat at my counting frame to assess the people,
from a farmer a tithe, a merchant a fifth of his gain,
marking the register, listening to their lies,
a bushel of dried apricots, marking the register,
three rolls of Egyptian cloth, astute in their avarice;
with Abdoel squatting before piled pence,
counting and calling the sum,
ringing and weighing coin,
casting one out, four or five of a score,
calling the deficit;
one stood in the door
scorning our occupation,
silent: so in his greaves I saw
in polished bronze
a man like me reckoning pence,
never having tasted bread
where there is ice in his flask,
storks' stilts cleaving sun-disk,
sun like driven sand.
Camels raise their necks from the ground,
cooks scour kettles, soldiers oil their arms,
snow lights up high over the north,
yellow spreads in the desert, driving blue westward
among banks, surrounding patches of blue,
advancing in enemy land.
Kettles flash, bread is eaten,
scarabs are scurrying rolling dung.
Thirty gorged vultures on an ass's carcass

29

jostle, stumble, flop aside, drunk with flesh,
too heavy to fly, wings deep with inner gloss.
Lean watches, then debauch:
after long alert, stupidity:
waking, soar. If here you find me
intrusive and dangerous, seven years was I bonded
for Leah, seven toiled for Rachel:
now in a brothel outside under the wall
have paused to bait on my journey.
Another shall pay the bill if I can evade it.

LUD:
When Tigris floods snakes swarm in the city,
coral, jade, jet, between jet and jade, yellow,
enamelled toys. Toads
crouch on doorsteps. Jerboas
weary, unwary, may be taught to feed
from a fingertip. Dead camels, dead Kurds,
unmanageable rafts of logs
hinder the ferryman, a pull and a grunt,
a stiff tow upshore against the current.
Naked boys among water-buffaloes,
daughters without smile
treading clothes by the verge,
harsh smouldering dung:
a woman taking bread from her oven
spreads dates, an onion, cheese.
Silence under the high sun. When the ewes go out
along the towpath striped with palm-trunk shadows
a herdsman pipes, a girl shrills
under her load of greens. There is no clamour
in our market, no eagerness for gain;
even whores surly, God frugal,
keeping tale of prayers.

ARPACHSHAD:
Bound to beasts' udders, rags no dishonour,
not by much intercourse ennobled,
multitude of books, bought deference:
meagre flesh tingling to a mouthful of water,
apt to no servitude, commerce or special dexterity,
at night after prayers recite the sacred

30

enscrolled poems, beating with a leaping measure
like blood in a new wound:
These were the embers . . . Halt, both, lament . . . :
moon-silver on sand-pale gold,
plash against parched Arabia.
What's to dismay us?

ARAM:

By the dategroves of Babylon
there we sat down and sulked
while they were seeking to hire us
to a repugnant trade.
Are there no plows in Judah, seed or a sickle,
no ewe to the pail, press to the vineyard?
Sickly our Hebrew voices far from the Hebrew hills!

ASSHUR:

We bear witness against the merchants of Babylon
that they have planted ink and reaped figures.

LUD:

Against the princes of Babylon, that they have tithed of the best
leaving sterile ram, weakly hogg to the flock.

ARPACHSHAD:

Fullers, tailors, hairdressers, jewellers, perfumers.

ARAM:

David dancing before the Ark, they toss him pennies.
A farthing a note for songs as of the thrush.

ASSHUR:

Golden skin scoured in sandblast
a vulture's wing. 'Soldier,
O soldier! Hard muscles, nipples like spikes.
Undo the neck-string, let my blue gown fall.'
Very much like going to bed with a bronze.
The child cradled beside her sister silent and brown.
Thighs in a sunshaft, uncontrollable smile,
she tossed the pence aside in a brothel under the wall.

LUD:

My bride is borne behind the pipers,
kettles and featherbed,
on her forehead jet, jade, coral under the veil;
to bring ewes to the pail, bread from the oven.
Breasts scarcely hump her smock,
thighs meagre, eyes
alert without smile
mock the beribboned dancing boys.

ARPACHSHAD:

Drunk with her flesh when, polished leather,
still as moon she fades into the sand,
spurts a flame in the abandoned embers,
gold on silver. Warmth of absent thighs
dies on the loins: she who has yet no breasts
and no patience to await tomorrow.

ARAM:

Chattering in the vineyard,
breasts swelled, halt and beweep
captives, sickly, closing repugnant thighs.
Who lent her warmth to dying David, let her seed
sleep on the Hebrew hills, wake under Zion.

What's begotten on a journey but souvenirs?
Life we give and take, pence in a market,
without noting beggar, dealer, changer;
pence we drop in the sawdust with spilt wine.

II

They filled the eyes of the vaulting
with alabaster panes,
each pencil of arches spouting
from a short pier,
and whitewashed the whole, using
a thread of blue to restore
lines nowhere broken,
for they considered capital
and base irrelevant.
The light is sufficient
to perceive the motions of prayer
and the place cool.
Tiles for domes and aivans
they baked in a corner,
older, where Avicenna may have worshipped.
The south dome, Nezam-ol-Molk's,
grows without violence from the walls
of a square chamber. Taj-ol-Molk
set a less perfect dome
over a forest of pillars.
At Veramin
Malekshah cut his pride in plaster
which hardens by age, the same
who found Khayyam a better reckoner
than the Author of the Qor'an.
Their passion's body was bricks and its soul algebra.
Poetry
they remembered
too much, too well.
'Lately a professor in this university'
said Khayyam of a recalcitrant ass,
'therefore would not enter, dare not face me.'
But their determination to banish fools foundered
ultimately in the installation of absolute idiots.
Fear of being imputed
naive impeded thought.
Eddies both ways in time:
the builders of La Giralda
repeated

heavily, languidly,
some of their patterns in brick.
I wonder what Khayyam thought
of all the construction and organisation afoot,
foreigners, resolute Seljuks, not so bloodthirsty
as some benefactors of mankind; recalling
perhaps Abu Ali's horror of munificent patrons;
books unheard of or lost elsewhere
in the library at Bokhara,
and four hours writing a day
before the duties of prime minister.

For all that, the Seljuks avoided
Roman exaggeration and the leaden mind of Egypt
and withered precariously on the bough
with patience and public spirit.
O public spirit!

Prayers to band cities and brigade men
lest there be more wills than one:
but God is the dividing sword.

A hard pyramid or lasting law
against fear of death and
murder more durable than mortar.

Domination and engineers
to fudge a motive you can lay your hands on
lest a girl choose or refuse waywardly.

From Hajji Mosavvor's trembling wrist
grace of tree and beast
shines on ivory
in eloquent line.
Flute,
shade dimples under chenars
breath of Naystani chases and traces
as a pair of gods might dodge and tag between stars.
Taj is to sing, Taj,
when tar and drum
come to their silence, slow,

clear, rich, as though
he had cadence and phrase from Hafez.
Nothing that was is,
but Moluk-e-Zarrabi
draws her voice from a well
deeper than history.
Shir-e Khoda's note
on a dawn-cold radio
forestalls, outlasts the beat.
Friday, Sobhi's tales
keeping boys from their meat.

A fowler spreading his net
over the barley, calls,
calls on a rubber reed.
Grain nods in reply.
Poppies blue upon white
wake to the sun's frown.
Scut of gazelle dances and bounces
out of the afternoon.
Owl and wolf to the night.
On a terrace over a pool
vafur, vodka, tea,
resonant verse spilled
from Onsori, Sa'di,
till the girls' mutter is lost
in whisper of stream and leaf,
a final nightingale
under a fading sky
azan on their quiet.

They despise police work,
are not masters of filing:
always a task for foreigners
to make them unhappy,
unproductive and rich.

Have you seen a falcon stoop
accurate, unforseen
and absolute, between
wind-ripples over harvest? Dread

of what's to be, is and has been—
were we not better dead?

His wings churn air
to flight.
Feathers alight
with sun, he rises where
dazzle rebuts our stare,
wonder our fright.

III

All things only of earth and water,
to sit in the sun's warmth
breathing clear air.
A fancy took me to dig,
plant, prune, graft;
milk, skim, churn;
flay and tan.
A side of salt beef
for a knife chased and inscribed.
A cask of pressed grapes
for a seine-net.
For peace until harvest
a jig and a hymn.

How shall wheat sprout
through a shingle of Lydian pebbles
that turn the harrow's points?
Quarry and build, Solomon,
a bank for Lydian pebbles:
tribute of Lydian pebbles
levy and lay aside,
that twist underfoot
and blunt the plowshare,
countless, useless, hampering
pebbles that spawn.

Shot silk and damask white
spray spread from
artesian gush of our past.
Let no one drink unchlorinated
living water but taxed tap, sterile,
or seek his contraband mouthful
in bog, under thicket, by crag, a trickle,
or from embroidered pools
with newts and dytiscus beetles.

One cribbed in a madhouse
set about with diagnoses;
one unvisited; one uninvited;

one visited and invited too much;
one impotent, suffocated by adulation;
one unfed: flares on a foundering barque,
stars spattering still sea under iceblink.

Tinker tapping perched on a slagheap
and the man who can mend a magneto.
Flight-lieutenant Idema, half course run
that started from Grand Rapids, Michigan,
wouldnt fight for Roosevelt,
'that bastard Roosevelt', pale
at Malta's ruins, enduring
a jeep guarded like a tyrant.
In British uniform and pay
for fun of fighting and pride,
for Churchill on foot alone,
clowning with a cigar, was lost
in best blues and his third plane that day.

Broken booty but usable
along the littoral, frittering into the south.
We marvelled, careful of craters and minefields,
noting a new-painted recognisance
on a fragment of fuselage, sand drifting into dumps,
a tank's turret twisted skyward,
here and there a lorry unharmed
out of fuel or the crew scattered;
leaguered in lines numbered for enemy units,
gulped beer of their brewing,
mocked them marching unguarded to our rear;
discerned nothing indigenous, never a dwelling,
but on the shore sponges stranded and beyond the reef
unstayed masts staggering in the swell,
till we reached readymade villages clamped on cornland,
empty, Arabs feeding vines to goats;
at last orchards aligned, girls hawked by their mothers
from tent to tent, Tripoli dark
under a cone of tracers.
Old in that war after raising many crosses
rapped on a tomb at Leptis; no one opened.

Blind Bashshar bin Burd saw,
doubted, glanced back,
guessed whence, speculated whither.
Panegyrists, blinder and deaf,
prophets, exegesists, counsellors of patience
lie in wait for blood,
every man with a net.
Condole with me with abundance of secret pleasure.
What we think in private
will be said in public
before the last gallon's teemed
into an unintelligible sea—
old men who toil in the bilge to open a link,
bruised by the fling of the ship and sodden
sleep at the handpump. Staithes, filthy harbour water,
a drowned Finn, a drowned Chinee;
hard-lying money wrung from protesting paymasters.

Rosyth guns sang. Sang tide through cable
for Glasgow burning:
            'Bright west,
              pale east,
                catfish on the sprool.'
Sun leaped up and passed,
bolted towards green creek
of quiet Chesapeake,
bight of a warp no strong tide strains. Yet
as tea's drawing, breeze backing and freshening,
who'd rather
make fast Fortune with a slippery hitch?
Tide sang. Guns sang:
            'Vigilant,
              pull off fluffed woollens, strip
                to buff and beyond.'
In watch below
meditative heard elsewhere
surf shout, pound shores seldom silent
from which heart naked swam
out to the dear unintelligible ocean.

From Largo Law look down,
moon and dry weather, look down
on convoy marshalled, filing between mines.
Cold northern clear sea-gardens
between Lofoten and Spitzbergen,
as good a grave as any, earth or water.
What else do we live for and take part,
we who would share the spoils?

1951

BRIGGFLATTS

An Autobiography

For Peggy

Son los pasariellos del mal pelo exidos

The spuggies are fledged

I

Brag, sweet tenor bull,
descant on Rawthey's madrigal,
each pebble its part
for the fells' late spring.
Dance tiptoe, bull,
black against may.
Ridiculous and lovely
chase hurdling shadows
morning into noon.
May on the bull's hide
and through the dale
furrows fill with may,
paving the slowworm's way.

A mason times his mallet
to a lark's twitter,
listening while the marble rests,
lays his rule
at a letter's edge,
fingertips checking,
till the stone spells a name
naming none,
a man abolished.
Painful lark, labouring to rise!
The solemn mallet says:
In the grave's slot
he lies. We rot.

Decay thrusts the blade,
wheat stands in excrement
trembling. Rawthey trembles.
Tongue stumbles, ears err
for fear of spring.
Rub the stone with sand,
wet sandstone rending
roughness away. Fingers
ache on the rubbing stone.
The mason says: Rocks
happen by chance.
No one here bolts the door,
love is so sore.

Stone smooth as skin,
cold as the dead they load
on a low lorry by night.
The moon sits on the fell
but it will rain.
Under sacks on the stone
two children lie,
hear the horse stale,
the mason whistle,
harness mutter to shaft,
felloe to axle squeak,
rut thud the rim,
crushed grit.

Stocking to stocking, jersey to jersey,
head to a hard arm,
they kiss under the rain,
bruised by their marble bed.
In Garsdale, dawn;
at Hawes, tea from the can.
Rain stops, sacks
steam in the sun, they sit up.
Copper-wire moustache,
sea-reflecting eyes
and Baltic plainsong speech
declare: By such rocks
men killed Bloodaxe.

Fierce blood throbs in his tongue,
lean words.
Skulls cropped for steel caps
huddle round Stainmore.
Their becks ring on limestone,
whisper to peat.
The clogged cart pushes the horse downhill.
In such soft air
they trudge and sing,
laying the tune frankly on the air.
All sounds fall still,
fellside bleat,
hide-and-seek peewit.

44

Her pulse their pace,
palm countering palm,
till a trench is filled,
stone white as cheese
jeers at the dale.
Knotty wood, hard to rive,
smoulders to ash;
smell of October apples.
The road again,
at a trot.
Wetter, warmed, they watch
the mason meditate
on name and date.

Rain rinses the road,
the bull streams and laments.
Sour rye porridge from the hob
with cream and black tea,
meat, crust and crumb.
Her parents in bed
the children dry their clothes.
He has untied the tape
of her striped flannel drawers
before the range. Naked
on the pricked rag mat
his fingers comb
thatch of his manhood's home.

Gentle generous voices weave
over bare night
words to confirm and delight
till bird dawn.
Rainwater from the butt
she fetches and flannel
to wash him inch by inch,
kissing the pebbles.
Shining slowworm part of the marvel.
The mason stirs:
Words!
Pens are too light.
Take a chisel to write.

Every birth a crime,
every sentence life.
Wiped of mould and mites
would the ball run true?
No hope of going back.
Hounds falter and stray,
shame deflects the pen.
Love murdered neither bleeds nor stifles
but jogs the draftsman's elbow.
What can he, changed, tell
her, changed, perhaps dead?
Delight dwindles. Blame
stays the same.

Brief words are hard to find,
shapes to carve and discard:
Bloodaxe, king of York,
king of Dublin, king of Orkney.
Take no notice of tears;
letter the stone to stand
over love laid aside lest
insufferable happiness impede
flight to Stainmore,
to trace
lark, mallet,
becks, flocks
and axe knocks.

Dung will not soil the slowworm's
mosaic. Breathless lark
drops to nest in sodden trash;
Rawthey truculent, dingy.
Drudge at the mallet, the may is down,
fog on fells. Guilty of spring
and spring's ending
amputated years ache after
the bull is beef, love a convenience.
It is easier to die than to remember.
Name and date
split in soft slate
a few months obliterate.

II

Poet appointed dare not decline
to walk among the bogus, nothing to authenticate
the mission imposed, despised
by toadies, confidence men, kept boys,
shopped and jailed, cleaned out by whores,
touching acquaintance for food and tobacco.
Secret, solitary, a spy, he gauges
lines of a Flemish horse
hauling beer, the angle, obtuse,
a slut's blouse draws on her chest,
counts beat against beat, bus conductor
against engine against wheels against
the pedal, Tottenham Court Road, decodes
thunder, scans
porridge bubbling, pipes clanking, feels
Buddha's basalt cheek
but cannot name the ratio of its curves
to the half-pint
left breast of a girl who bared it in Kleinfeldt's.
He lies with one to long for another,
sick, self-maimed, self-hating,
obstinate, mating
beauty with squalor to beget lines still-born.

You who can calculate the course
of a biased bowl,
shall I come near the jack?
What twist can counter the force
that holds back
woods I roll?

You who elucidate the disk
hubbed by the sun,
shall I see autumn out
or the fifty years at risk
be lost, doubt
end what's begun?

Under his right oxter the loom of his sweep
the pilot turns from the wake.

Thole-pins shred where the oar leans,
grommets renewed, tallowed;
halliards frapped to the shrouds.
Crew grunt and gasp. Nothing he sees
they see, but hate and serve. Unscarred ocean,
day's swerve, swell's poise, pursuit,
he blends, balances, drawing leagues under the keel
to raise cold cliffs where tides
knot fringes of weed.
No tilled acre, gold scarce,
walrus tusk, whalebone, white bear's liver.
Scurvy gnaws, steading smell, hearth's crackle.
Crabs, shingle, seracs on the icefall.
Summer is bergs and fogs, lichen on rocks.
Who cares to remember a name cut in ice
or be remembered?
Wind writes in foam on the sea:

Who sang, sea takes,
brawn brine, bone grit.
Keener the kittiwake.
Fells forget him.
Fathoms dull the dale,
gulfweed voices . . .

About ship! Sweat in the south. Go bare
because the soil is adorned,
sunset the colour of a boiled louse.
Steep sluice or level,
parts of the sewer ferment faster.
Days jerk, dawdle, fidget
towards the cesspit.
Love is a vapour, we're soon through it.

Flying fish follow the boat,
delicate wings blue, grace
on flick of a tissue tail,
the water's surface between
appetite and attainment.
Flexible, unrepetitive line
to sing, not paint; sing, sing,
laying the tune on the air,

nimble and easy as a lizard,
still and sudden as a gecko,
to humiliate love, remember
nothing.

It tastes good, garlic and salt in it,
with the half-sweet white wine of Orvieto
on scanty grass under great trees
where the ramparts cuddle Lucca.

It sounds right, spoken on the ridge
between marine olives and hillside
blue figs, under the breeze fresh
with pollen of Apennine sage.

It feels soft, weed thick in the cave
and the smooth wet riddance of Antonietta's
bathing suit, mouth ajar for
submarine Amalfitan kisses.

It looks well on the page, but never
well enough. Something is lost
when wind, sun, sea upbraid
justly an unconvinced deserter.

White marble stained like a urinal
cleft in Apuan Alps,
always trickling, apt to the saw. Ice and wedge
split it or well-measured cordite shots,
while paraffin pistons rap, saws rip
and clamour is clad in stillness:
clouds echo marble middens, sugar-white,
that cumber the road stones travel
to list the names of the dead.
There is a lot of Italy in churchyards,
sea on the left, the Garfagnana
over the wall, la Cisa flaking
to hillside fiddlers above Parma,
melancholy, swift,
with light bow blanching the dance.
Grease mingles with sweat
on the threshing floor. Frogs, grasshoppers

drape the rice in sound.
Tortoise deep in dust or
muzzled bear capering
punctuate a text whose initial,
lost in Lindisfarne plaited lines,
stands for discarded love.

Win from rock
    flame and ore.
Crucibles pour
    sanded ingots.

Heat and hammer
    draw out a bar.
Wheel and water
    grind an edge.

No worn tool
    whittles stone;
but a reproached
    uneasy mason

shaping evasive
    ornament
litters his yard
    with flawed fragments.

Loaded with mail of linked lies,
what weapon can the king lift to fight
when chance-met enemies employ sly
sword and shoulder-piercing pike,
pressed into the mire,
trampled and hewn till a knife
—in whose hand?—severs tight
neck cords? Axe rusts. Spine
picked bare by ravens, agile
maggots devour the slack side
and inert brain, never wise.
What witnesses he had life,
ravelled and worn past splice,
yarns falling to staple? Rime
on the bent, the beck ice,

there will be nothing on Stainmore to hide
void, no sable to disguise
what he wore under the lies,
king of Orkney, king of Dublin, twice
king of York, where the tide
stopped till long flight
from who knows what smile,
scowl, disgust or delight
ended in bale on the fellside.

Starfish, poinsettia on a half-tide crag,
a galliard by Byrd.
Anemones spite cullers of ornament
but design the pool
to their grouping. The hermit crab
is no grotesque in such company.

Asian vultures riding on a spiral
column of dust
or swift desert ass startled by the
camels' dogged saunter
figures sudden flight of the descant
on a madrigal by Monteverdi.

But who will entune a bogged orchard,
its blossom gone,
fruit unformed, where hunger and
damp hush the hive?
A disappointed July full of codling
moth and ragged lettuces?

Yet roe are there, rise to the fence, insolent;
a scared vixen cringes
red against privet stems as a mazurka;
and rat, grey, rummaging
behind the compost heap has daring
to thread, lithe and alert, Schoenberg's maze.

Riding silk, adrift on noon,
a spider gleams like a berry
less black than cannibal slug
but no less pat under elders

where shadows themselves are a web.
So is summer held to its contract
and the year solvent; but men
driven by storm fret,
reminded of sweltering Crete
and Pasiphae's pungent sweat,
who heard the god-bull's feet
scattering sand,
breathed byre stink, yet stood
with expectant hand
to guide his seed to its soil;
nor did flesh flinch
distended by the brute
nor loaded spirit sink
till it had gloried in unlike creation.

III

Down into dust and reeds
at the patrolled bounds
where captives thicken to gaze
slither companions, wary, armed,
whose torches straggle
seeking charred hearths
to define a road.
Day, dim, laps at the shore
in petulant ripples
soon smoothed in night
on pebbles worn by tabulation till
only the shell of figures is left
as fragile honeycomb breeze.
Tides of day strew the shingle
tides of night sweep, snoring;
and some turned back, taught
by dreams the year would capsize
where the bank quivers, paved
with gulls stunned on a cliff
not hard to climb, muffled
in flutter, scored by beaks,
pestered by scavengers
whose palms scoop droppings to mould
cakes for hungry towns. One
plucked fruit warm from the arse
of his companion, who
making to beat him, he screamed:
Hastor! Hastor! but Hastor
raised dung thickened lashes to stare
disdaining those who cry:
Sweet shit! Buy!
for he swears in the market:
By God with whom I lunched!
there is no trash in the wheat
my loaf is kneaded from.
Nor will unprofitable motion
stir the stink that settles round him.
Leave given
we would have slaughtered the turd-bakers
but neither whip nor knife

can welt their hide.
Guides at the top claim fees
though the way is random
past hovels hags lean from
rolling lizard eyes
at boys gnawed by the wolf,
past bevelled downs, grey marshes
where some souse in brine
long rotted corpses, others,
needier, sneak through saltings
to snatch toe, forearm, ear,
and on gladly to hills
briar and bramble vest
where beggars advertise
rash, chancre, fistula,
to hug glib shoulders, mingle herpetic
limbs with stumps and cosset the mad.
Some the Laughing Stone disables
whom giggle and snicker waste
till fun suffocates them. Beyond
we heard the teeming falls of the dead,
saw kelts fall back long-jawed, without flesh,
cruel by appetite beyond its term,
straining to bright gravel spawning pools.
Eddies batter them, borne down to the sea,
archipelago of galaxies,
zero suspending the world.
Banners purple and green flash from its walls,
pennants of red, orange blotched pale on blue,
glimmer of ancient arms
to pen and protect mankind.
But we desired Macedonia,
the rocky meadows, horses, barley pancakes,
incest and familiar games,
to end in our place by our own wars,
and deemed the peak unscaleable; but he
reached to a crack in the rock
with some scorn, resolute though in doubt,
traversed limestone to gabbro,
file sharp, skinning his fingers,
and granite numb with ice, in air
too thin to bear up a gnat,

scrutinising holds while day lasted,
groping for holds in the dark
till the morning star reflected
in the glazed crag
and other light not of the sun
dawning from above
lit feathers sweeping snow
and the limbs of Israfel,
trumpet in hand, intent on the east,
cheeks swollen to blow,
whose sigh is cirrus: Yet delay!
When will the signal come
to summon man to his clay?

Heart slow, nerves numb and memory, he lay
on glistening moss by a spring;
as a woodman dazed by an adder's sting
barely within recall
tests the rebate tossed to him, so he
ascertained moss and bracken,
a cold squirm snaking his flank
and breath leaked to his ear:
I am neither snake nor lizard,
I am the slowworm.

Ripe wheat is my lodging. I polish
my side on pillars of its transept,
gleam in its occasional light.
Its swaying
copies my gait.

Vaults stored with slugs to relish,
my quilt a litter of husks, I prosper
lying low, little concerned.
My eyes sharpen
when I blink.

Good luck to reaper and miller!
Grubs adhere even to stubble.
Come plowtime
the ditch is near.

Sycamore seed twirling,
O, writhe to its measure!
Dust swirling trims pleasure.
Thorns prance in a gale.
In air snow flickers,
twigs tap,
elms drip.

Swaggering, shimmering fall,
drench and towel us all!

So he rose and led home silently through clean woodland
where every bough repeated the slowworm's song.

IV

Grass caught in willow tells the flood's height that has subsided;
overfalls sketch a ledge to be bared tomorrow.
No angler homes with empty creel though mist dims day.
I hear Aneurin number the dead, his nipped voice.
Slight moon limps after the sun. A closing door
stirs smoke's flow above the grate. Jangle
to skald, battle, journey; to priest Latin is bland.
Rats have left no potatoes fit to roast, the gamey tang
recalls ibex guts steaming under a cold ridge,
tomcat stink of a leopard dying while I stood
easing the bolt to dwell on a round's shining rim.
I hear Aneurin number the dead and rejoice,
being adult male of a merciless species.
Today's posts are piles to drive into the quaggy past
on which impermanent palaces balance.
I see Aneurin's pectoral muscle swell under his shirt,
pacing between the game Ida left to rat and raven,
young men, tall yesterday, with cabled thighs.
Red deer move less warily since their bows dropped.
Girls in Teesdale and Wensleydale wake discontent.
Clear Cymric voices carry well this autumn night,
Aneurin and Taliesin, cruel owls
for whom it is never altogether dark, crying
before the rules made poetry a pedant's game.
Columba, Columbanus, as the soil shifts its vest,
Aidan and Cuthbert put on daylight,
wires of sharp western metal entangled in its soft
web, many shuttles as midges darting;
not for bodily welfare nor pauper theorems
but splendour to splendour, excepting nothing that is.
Let the fox have his fill, patient leech and weevil,
cattle refer the rising of Sirius to their hedge horizon,
runts murder the sacred calves of the sea by rule
heedless of herring gull, surf and the text carved by waves
on the skerry. Can you trace shuttles thrown
like drops from a fountain, spray, mist of spiderlines
bearing the rainbow, quoits round the draped moon;
shuttles like random dust desert whirlwinds hoy at their
                                        tormenting sun?
Follow the clue patiently and you will understand nothing.

Lice in its seams despise the jacket shrunk to the world's core,
crawl with toil to glimpse
from its shoulder walls of flame which could they reach
they'd crackle like popcorn in a skillet.

As the player's breath warms the fipple the tone clears.
It is time to consider how Domenico Scarlatti
condensed so much music into so few bars
with never a crabbed turn or congested cadence,
never a boast or a see-here; and stars and lakes
echo him and the copse drums out his measure,
snow peaks are lifted up in moonlight and twilight
and the sun rises on an acknowledged land.

My love is young but wise. Oak, applewood,
her fire is banked with ashes till day.
The fells reek of her hearth's scent,
her girdle is greased with lard;
hunger is stayed on her settle, lust in her bed.
Light as spider floss her hair on my cheek which a puff scatters,
light as a moth her fingers on my thigh.
We have eaten and loved and the sun is up,
we have only to sing before parting:
Goodbye, dear love.

Her scones are greased with fat of fried bacon,
her blanket comforts my belly like the south.
We have eaten and loved and the sun is up.
Goodbye.

Applewood, hard to rive,
its knots smoulder all day.
Cobweb hair on the morning,
a puff would blow it away.
Rime is crisp on the bent,
ruts stone-hard, frost spangles fleece.
What breeze will fill that sleeve limp on the line?
A boy's jet steams from the wall, time from the year,
care from deed and undoing.
Shamble, cold, content with beer and pickles,
towards a taciturn lodging amongst strangers.

Where rats go go I,
accustomed to penury,
filth, disgust and fury;
evasive to persist,
reject the bait
yet gnaw the best.
My bony feet
sully shelf and dresser,
keeping a beat in the dark,
rap on lath
till dogs bark
and sleep, shed,
slides from the bed.
O valiant when hunters
with stick and terrier bar escape
or wavy ferret leaps,
encroach and cede again,
rat, roommate, unreconciled.

Stars disperse. We too,
further from neighbours
now the year ages.

V

Drip—icicle's gone.
Slur, ratio, tone,
chime dilute what's done
as a flute clarifies song,
trembling phrase fading to pause
then glow. Solstice past,
years end crescendo.

Winter wrings pigment
from petal and slough
but thin light lays
white next red on sea-crow wing,
gruff sole cormorant
whose grief turns carnival.
Even a bangle of birds
to bind sleeve to wrist
as west wind waves to east
a just perceptible greeting—
sinews ripple the weave,
threads flex, slew, hues meeting,
parting in whey-blue haze.

Mist sets lace of frost
on rock for the tide to mangle.
Day is wreathed in what summer lost.

Conger skimped at the ebb, lobster,
neither will I take, nor troll
roe of its like for salmon.
Let bass sleep, gentles
brisk, skim-grey,
group a nosegay
jostling on cast flesh,
frisk and compose decay
to side shot with flame,
unresting bluebottle wing. Sing,
strewing the notes on the air
as ripples skip in a shallow. Go
bare, the shore is adorned
with pungent weed loudly
filtering sand and sea.

Silver blades of surf
fall crisp on rustling grit,
shaping the shore as a mason
fondles and shapes his stone.

Shepherds follow the links,
sweet turf studded with thrift;
fell-born men of precise instep
leading demure dogs
from Tweed and Till and Teviotdale,
with hair combed back from the muzzle,
dogs from Redesdale and Coquetdale
taught by Wilson or Telfer.
Their teeth are white as birch,
slow under black fringe
of silent, accurate lips.
The ewes are heavy with lamb.
Snow lies bright on Hedgehope
and tacky mud about Till
where the fells have stepped aside
and the river praises itself,
silence by silence sits
and Then is diffused in Now.

Light lifts from the water.
Frost has put rowan down,
a russet blotch of bracken
tousled about the trunk.
Bleached sky. Cirrus
reflects sun that has left
nothing to badger eyes.

Young flutes, harps touched by a breeze,
drums and horns escort
Aldebaran, low in the clear east,
beckoning boats to the fishing.
Capella floats from the north
with shields hung on his gunwale.
That is no dinghy's lantern
occulted by the swell—Betelgeuse,
calling behind him to Rigel.
Starlight is almost flesh.

Great strings next the post of the harp
clang, the horn has majesty,
flutes flicker in the draft and flare.
Orion strides over Farne.
Seals shuffle and bark,
terns shift on their ledges,
watching Capella steer for the zenith,
and Procyon starts his climb.

Furthest, fairest things, stars, free of our humbug,
each his own, the longer known the more alone,
wrapt in emphatic fire roaring out to a black flue.
Each spark trills on a tone beyond chronological compass,
yet in a sextant's bubble present and firm
places a surveyor's stone or steadies a tiller.
Then is Now. The star you steer by is gone,
its tremulous thread spun in the hurricane
spider floss on my cheek; light from the zenith
spun when the slowworm lay in her lap
fifty years ago.

The sheets are gathered and bound,
the volume indexed and shelved,
dust on its marbled leaves.
Lofty, an empty combe,
silent but for bees.
Finger tips touched and were still
fifty years ago.
Sirius is too young to remember.

Sirius glows in the wind. Sparks on ripples
mark his line, lures for spent fish.

Fifty years a letter unanswered;
a visit postponed for fifty years.

She has been with me fifty years.

Starlight quivers. I had day enough.
For love uninterrupted night.

CODA

A strong song tows
us, long earsick.
Blind, we follow
rain slant, spray flick
to fields we do not know.

Night, float us.
Offshore wind, shout,
ask the sea
what's lost, what's left,
what horn sunk,
what crown adrift.

Where we are who knows
of kings who sup
while day fails? Who,
swinging his axe
to fell kings, guesses
where we go?

1965

CHOMEI AT TOYAMA

CHOMEI AT TOYAMA

(Kamo-no-Chomei, born at Kamo 1154, died at Toyama on Mount Hino, 24th June 1216)

Swirl sleeping in the waterfall!
On motionless pools scum appearing
                              disappearing!

Eaves formal on the zenith,
lofty city Kyoto,
wealthy, without antiquities!

Housebreakers clamber about,
builders raising floor upon floor
at the corner sites, replacing
gardens by bungalows.

In the town where I was known
the young men stare at me.
A few faces I know remain.

Whence comes man at his birth? or where
does death lead him? Whom do you mourn?
Whose steps wake your delight?
Dewy hibiscus dries: though dew
outlast the petals.

I have been noting events forty years.

On the twentyseventh May eleven hundred
and seventyseven, eight p.m., fire broke out
at the corner of Tomi and Higuchi streets.
In a night
palace, ministries, university, parliament
were destroyed. As the wind veered
flames spread out in the shape of an open fan.
Tongues torn by gusts stretched and leapt.
In the sky clouds of cinders lit red with the blaze.

Some choked, some burned, some barely escaped.
Sixteen great officials lost houses and
very many poor. A third of the city burned;
several thousands died; and of beasts,
limitless numbers.

Men are fools to invest in real estate.

Three years less three days later a wind
starting near the outer boulevard
broke a path a quarter mile across
to Sixth Avenue.
Not a house stood. Some were felled whole,
some in splinters; some had left
great beams upright in the ground
and round about
lay rooves scattered where the wind flung them.
Flocks of furniture in the air,
everything flat fluttered like dead leaves.
A dust like fog or smoke,
you could hear nothing for the roar,
　　　　　bufera infernal!
Lamed some, wounded some.
This cyclone turned southwest.

Massacre without cause.

Portent?

The same year thunderbolted change of capital,
fixed here, Kyoto, for ages.
Nothing compelled the change nor was it an easy matter
but the grumbling was disproportionate.
We moved, those with jobs
or wanting jobs or hangers on of the rest,
in haste haste fretting to be the first.
Rooftrees overhanging empty rooms;
dismounted: floating down the river.
The soil returned to heath.

I visited the new site: narrow and too uneven,
cliffs and marshes, deafening shores, perpetual strong winds;

the palace a logcabin dumped amongst the hills
(yet not altogether inelegant).
There was no flat place for houses, many vacant lots,
the former capital wrecked, the new a camp,
and thoughts like clouds changing, frayed by a breath:
peasants bewailing lost land, newcomers aghast at prices.
No one in uniform: the crowds
resembled demobilized conscripts.

There were murmurs. Time defined them.
In the winter the decree was rescinded,
we returned to Kyoto;
but the houses were gone and none
could afford to rebuild them.

I have heard of a time when kings beneath bark rooves
watched chimneys.
When smoke was scarce, taxes were remitted.

To appreciate present conditions
collate them with those of antiquity.

Drought, floods, and a dearth. Two fruitless autumns.
Empty markets, swarms of beggars. Jewels
sold for a handful of rice. Dead stank
on the curb, lay so thick on
Riverside Drive a car couldnt pass.
The pest bred.
That winter my fuel was the walls of my own house.

Fathers fed their children and died,
babies died sucking the dead.
The priest Hoshi went about marking their foreheads
A, Amida, their requiem;
he counted them in the East End in the last two months,
fortythree thousand A's.

Crack, rush, ye mountains, bury your rills!
Spread your green glass, ocean, over the meadows!
Scream, avalanche, boulders amok, strangle the dale!
O ships in the sea's power, O horses
on shifting roads, in the earth's power, without hoofhold!

69

This is the earthquake, this was
the great earthquake of Genryaku!

The chapel fell, the abbey, the minster and the small shrines
fell, their dust rose and a thunder of houses falling.
O to be birds and fly or dragons and ride on a cloud!
The earthquake, the great earthquake of Genryaku!

A child building a mud house against a high wall:
I saw him crushed suddenly, his eyes hung
from their orbits like two tassels.
His father howled shamelessly—an officer.
I was not abashed at his crying.

Such shocks continued three weeks; then lessening,
but still a score daily as big as an average earthquake;
then fewer, alternate days, a tertian ague of tremors.
There is no record of any greater.
It caused a religious revival.
Months . . .
Years . . .
. . . .
Nobody mentions it now.

This is the unstable world and
we in it unstable and our houses.

A poor man living amongst the rich
gives no rowdy parties, doesnt sing.
Dare he keep his child at home, keep a dog?
He dare not pity himself above a whimper.

But he visits, he flatters, he is put in his place,
he remembers the patch on his trousers.
His wife and sons despise him for being poor.
He has no peace.

If he lives in an alley of rotting frame houses
he dreads a fire.
If he commutes he loses his time
and leaves his house daily to be plundered by gunmen.

The bureaucrats are avaricious.
He who has no relatives in the Inland Revenue,
poor devil!

Whoever helps him enslaves him
and follows him crying out: *Gratitude!*
If he wants success he is wretched.
If he doesnt he passes for mad.

Where shall I settle, what trade choose
that the mind may practise, the body rest?

My grandmother left me a house
but I was always away
for my health and because I was alone there.
When I was thirty I couldnt stand it any longer,
I built a house to suit myself:
one bamboo room, you would have thought it a cartshed,
poor shelter from snow or wind.
It stood on the flood plain. And that quarter
is also flooded with gangsters.

One generation
I saddened myself with idealistic philosophies,
but before I was fifty
I perceived there was no time to lose,
left home and conversation.
Among the cloudy mountains of Ohara
spring and autumn, spring and autumn, spring and autumn,
emptier than ever.

The dew evaporates from my sixty years,
I have built my last house, or hovel,
a hunter's bivouac, an old
silkworm's cocoon:
ten feet by ten, seven high: and I,
reckoning it a lodging not a dwelling,
omitted the usual foundation ceremony.

I have filled the frames with clay,
set hinges at the corners;
easy to take it down and carry it away

when I get bored with this place.
Two barrowloads of junk
and the cost of a man to shove the barrow,
no trouble at all.

Since I have trodden Hino mountain
noon has beaten through the awning
over my bamboo balcony, evening
shone on Amida.
I have shelved my books above the window,
lute and mandolin near at hand,
piled bracken and a little straw for bedding,
a smooth desk where the light falls, stove for bramblewood.
I have gathered stones, fitted
stones for a cistern, laid bamboo
pipes. No woodstack,
wood enough in the thicket.

Toyama, snug in the creepers!
Toyama, deep in the dense gully, open
westward whence the dead ride out of Eden
squatting on blue clouds of wistaria.
(Its scent drifts west to Amida.)

Summer? Cuckoo's *Follow, follow*—to
harvest Purgatory hill!
Fall? The nightgrasshopper will
shrill *Fickle life*!
Snow will thicken on the doorstep,
melt like a drift of sins.
No friend to break silence,
no one will be shocked if I neglect the rite.
There's a Lent of commandments kept
where there's no way to break them.

A ripple of white water after a boat,
shining water after the boats Mansami saw
rowing at daybreak
at Okinoya.
Between the maple leaf and the caneflower
murmurs the afternoon—Po Lo-tien
saying goodbye on the verge of Jinyo river.
(I am playing scales on my mandolin.)

Be limber, my fingers, I am going to play *Autumn Wind*
to the pines, I am going to play *Hastening Brook*
to the water. I am no player
but there's nobody listening,
I do it for my own amusement.

Sixteen and sixty, I and the gamekeeper's boy,
one zest and equal, chewing tsubana buds,
one zest and equal, persimmon, pricklypear,
ears of sweetcorn pilfered from Valley Farm.

The view from the summit: sky bent over Kyoto,
picnic villages, Fushimi and Toba:
a very economical way of enjoying yourself.
Thought runs along the crest, climbs Sumiyama;
beyond Kasatori it visits the great church,
goes on pilgrimage to Ishiyama (no need to foot it!)
or the graves of poets, of Semimaru who said:

> *Somehow or other*
> *we scuttle through a lifetime.*
> *Somehow or other*
> *neither palace nor straw-hut*
> *is quite satisfactory.*

Not emptyhanded, with cherryblossom, with red maple
as the season gives it to decorate my Buddha
or offer a sprig at a time to chancecomers, home!

A fine moonlit night,
I sit at the window with a headful of old verses.

Whenever a monkey howls there are tears on my cuff.

Those are fireflies that seem
the fishermen's lights
off Maki island.

A shower at dawn
sings
like the hillbreeze in the leaves.

At the pheasant's chirr I recall
my father and mother uncertainly.

I rake my ashes.

Chattering fire,
soon kindled, soon burned out,
fit wife for an old man!

Neither closed in one landscape
nor in one season
the mind moving in illimitable
recollection.

I came here for a month
five years ago.
There's moss on the roof.

And I hear Soanso's dead
back in Kyoto.
I have as much room as I need.

I know myself and mankind.
. . . .
I dont want to be bothered.

(You will make me editor
of the Imperial Anthology?
I dont want to be bothered.)

You build for your wife, children,
cousins and cousins' cousins.
You want a house to entertain in.

A man like me can have neither servants nor friends
in the present state of society.
If I did not build for myself
for whom should I build?

Friends fancy a rich man's riches,
friends suck up to a man in high office.
If you keep straight you will have no friends
but catgut and blossom in season.

Servants weigh out their devotion
in proportion to their perquisites.

74

What do they care for peace and quiet?
There are more pickings in town.

I sweep my own floor
—less fuss.
I walk; I get tired
but do not have to worry about a horse.

My hands and feet will not loiter
when I am not looking.
I will not overwork them.
Besides, it's good for my health.

My jacket's wistaria flax,
my blanket hemp,
berries and young greens
my food.

(Let it be quite understood,
all this is merely personal.
I am not preaching the simple life
to those who enjoy being rich.)

I am shifting rivermist, not to be trusted.
I do not ask anything extraordinary of myself.
I like a nap after dinner
and to see the seasons come round in good order.

Hankering, vexation and apathy,
that's the run of the world.
Hankering, vexation and apathy,
keeping a carriage wont cure it.

Keeping a man in livery
wont cure it. Keeping a private fortress
wont cure it. These things satisfy no craving.
Hankering, vexation and apathy . . .

I am out of place in the capital,
people take me for a beggar,
as you would be out of place in this sort of life,
you are so—I regret it—so welded to your vulgarity.

75

The moonshadow merges with darkness
on the cliffpath,
a tricky turn near ahead.

Oh! There's nothing to complain about.
Buddha says: 'None of the world is good.'
I am fond of my hut . . .

I have renounced the world;
have a saintly
appearance.

I do not enjoy being poor,
I've a passionate nature.
My tongue
clacked a few prayers.

1932

FIRST BOOK OF ODES

1

Weeping oaks grieve, chestnuts raise
mournful candles. Sad is spring
to perpetuate, sad to trace
immortalities never changing.

Weary on the sea
for sight of land
gazing past the coming wave we
see the same wave;

drift on merciless reiteration of years;
descry no death; but spring
is everlasting
resurrection.

1924

2

Farewell ye sequent graces
voided faces still evasive!
Silent leavetaking and mournful
as nightwanderings
in unlit rooms or where the glow
of wall-reflected streetlamp light
or hasty matches shadowed large
and crowded out by imps of night
glimmer on cascades of
fantom dancers.
Airlapped, silent muses of light,
cease to administer
poisons to dying memories to stir
pangs of old rapture, cease to conspire
reunions of inevitable seed
long blown barren sown gathered
haphazard to wither.

1924

3

I am agog for foam. Tumultuous come
with teeming sweetness to the bitter shore
tidelong unrinsed and midday parched and numb
with expectation. If the bright sky bore
with endless utterance of a single blue
unphrased, its restless immobility
infects the soul, which must decline into
an anguished and exact sterility
and waste away: then how much more the sea
trembling with alteration must perfect
our loneliness by its hostility.
The dear companionship of its elect
deepens our envy. Its indifference
haunts us to suicide. Strong memories
of sprayblown days exasperate impatience
to brief rebellion and emphasise
the casual impotence we sicken of.
But when mad waves spring, braceletted with foam,
towards us in the angriness of love
crying a strange name, tossing as they come
repeated invitations in the gay
exuberance of unexplained desire,
we can forget the sad splendour and play
at wilfulness until the gods require
renewed inevitable hopeless calm
and the foam dies and we again subside
into our catalepsy, dreaming foam,
while the dry shore awaits another tide.

1926

81

4

After the grimaces of capitulation
the universal face resumes its cunning, quick
to abandon the nocturnal elevation.
                    In repose majestic,
vile wakening, cowering under its tyrant
eager in stratagems to circumvent the harsh
performer of unveilings, revealer of gaunt
lurking anatomy, grin of diurnal farce;
yet when the fellow with the red-hot poker comes
truculently to torment our blisters, we vie
with one another to present scarified bums
to the iron, clutching sausages greedily.
O Sun! Should I invoke this scorn, participate
in the inconsequence of this defeat, or hide
in noctambulistic exile to penetrate
secrets that moon and stars and empty death deride?

1926

5

Empty vast days built in the waste memory seem a jail for
thoughts grown stale in the mind, tardy of birth, rank and
                                        inflexible:
love and slow selfpraise, even grief's cogency, all emotions
timetamed whimper and shame changes the past brought to no
                                        utterance.

Ten or ten thousand, does it much signify, Helen, how we
date fantasmal events, London or Troy? Let Polyhymnia
strong with cadence multiply song, voices enmeshed by music
respond bringing the savour of our sadness or delight again.

                                         1927

6

. . . As to my heart, that may as well be forgotten
or labelled: Owner will dispose of same
to a good home, refs. exchgd., h.&c.,
previous experience desired but not essential
or let on a short lease to suit convenience.

1927

7

The day being Whitsun we had pigeon for dinner;
but Richmond in the pitted river saw
mudmirrored mackintosh, a wet southwest
wiped and smeared dampness over Twickenham.

Pools on the bustop's buttoned tarpaulin.
Wimbledon, Wandsworth, Clapham, the Oval. 'Lo,
Westminster Palace where the asses jaw!'

Endless disappointed buckshee-hunt!
Suburb and city giftless garden and street,
and the sky alight of an evening stubborn
and mute by day and never *rei novae*
inter rudes artium homines.
                never a spark of sedition
amongst the uneducated workingmen.

1928

Each fettered ghost slips to his several grave.

Loud intolerant bells (the shrinking nightflower closes
tenderly round its stars to baulk their hectoring)
orate to deaf hills where the olive stirs and dozes
in easeless age, dim to farce of man's fashioning.

Shepherds away! They toll throngs to your solitude
and their inquisitive harangue will disembody
shames and delights, all private features of your mood,
flay out your latencies, sieve your hopes, fray your shoddy.

The distant gods enorbed in bright indifference
whom we confess creatures or abstracts of our spirit,
unadored, absorbed into the incoherence,
leave desiccated names: rabbits sucked by a ferret.

1928

9

Dear be still! Time's start of us lengthens slowly.
Bright round plentiful nights ripen and fall for us.
Those impatient thighs will be bruised soon enough.

Sniff the sweet narcotic distilled by coupled
skins; moist bodies relaxed, mild, unemotional.
Thrifty fools spoil love with their headlong desires.

Dally! Waste! Mock! Loll! till the chosen sloth fails,
huge gasps empty the loins shuddering chilly in
long accumulated delight's thunderstorm.

Rinsed in cool sleep day will renew the summer
lightnings. Leave it to me. Only a savage's
lusts explode slapbang at the first touch like bombs.

1929

10 CHORUS OF FURIES

Guarda, mi disse, le feroce Erine

Let us come upon him first as if in a dream,
anonymous triple presence,
memory made substance and tally of heart's rot:
then in the waking Now be demonstrable, seem
sole aspect of being's essence,
coffin to the living touch, self's Iscariot.
Then he will loath the year's recurrent long caress
without hope of divorce,
envying idiocy's apathy or the stress
of definite remorse.
He will lapse into a halflife lest the taut force
of the mind's eagerness
recall those fiends or new apparitions endorse
his excessive distress.
He will shrink, his manhood leave him, slough selfaware
the last skin of the flayed: despair.
He will nurse his terror carefully, uncertain
even of death's solace,
impotent to outpace
dispersion of the soul, disruption of the brain.

1929

11

To a Poet who advised me to preserve
my fragments and false starts

Narciss, my numerous cancellations prefer
slow limpness in the damp dustbins amongst the peel
tobacco-ash and ends spittoon lickings litter
of labels dry corks breakages and a great deal

of miscellaneous garbage picked over by
covetous dustmen and Salvation Army sneaks
to one review-rid month's printed ignominy,
the public detection of your decay, that reeks.

1929

An arles, an arles for my hiring,
O master of singers, an arlespenny!

—Well sung singer, said Apollo,
but in this trade we pay no wages.

I too was once a millionaire
(in Germany during the inflation:
when the train steamed into Holland
I had not enough for a bun.)

The Lady asked the Poet:
Why do you wear your raincoat in the drawing-room?
He answered: Not to show
my arse sticking out of my trousers.

His muse left him for a steady man.
Quaeret in trivio vocationem.

(he is cadging for drinks at the streetcorners.)

1929

Fearful symmetry

Muzzle and jowl and beastly brow,
bilious glaring eyes, tufted ears,
recidivous criminality in the slouch,
—This is not the latest absconding bankrupt
but a 'beautiful' tiger imported at great expense from
Kuala Lumpur.

7 photographers, 4 black-and-white artists and an R.A.
are taking his profitable likeness;
28 reporters and an essayist
are writing him up.
Sundry ladies think he is a darling
especially at mealtimes, observing
that a firm near the docks advertises replicas
fullgrown on approval for easy cash payments.

♂ Felis Tigris (Straits Settlements) (Bobo) takes exercise
up and down his cage before feeding
in a stench of excrements of great cats
indifferent to beauty or brutality.
He is said to have eaten several persons
but of course you can never be quite sure of these things.

1929

14 GIN THE GOODWIFE STINT

The ploughland has gone to bent
and the pasture to heather;
gin the goodwife stint,
she'll keep the house together.

Gin the goodwife stint
and the bairns hunger
the Duke can get his rent
one year longer.

The Duke can get his rent
and we can get our ticket
twa pund emigrant
on a C.P.R. packet.

1930

15

Nothing
substance utters or time
stills and restrains
joins design and

supple measure deftly
as thought's intricate polyphonic
score dovetails with the tread
sensuous things
keep in our consciousness.

Celebrate man's craft
and the word spoken in shapeless night, the
sharp tool paring away
waste and the forms
cut out of mystery!

When taut string's note
passes ears' reach or red rays or violet
fade, strong over unseen
forces the word
ranks and enumerates . . .

mimes clouds condensed
and hewn hills and bristling forests,
steadfast corn in its season
and the seasons
in their due array,

life of man's own body
and death . . .
          The sound thins into melody,
discourse narrowing, craft
failing, design
petering out.

Ears heavy to breeze of speech and
thud of the ictus.

1930

16

Molten pool, incandescent spilth of
deep cauldrons—and brighter nothing is—
cast and cold, your blazes extinct and
no turmoil nor peril left you,
rusty ingot, bleak paralysed blob!

1930

To Mina Loy

Now that sea's over that island
so that barely on a calm day sun sleeks
a patchwork hatching of combed weed
over stubble and fallow alike
I resent drowned blackthorn hedge, choked ditch,
gates breaking from rusty hinges,
the submerged copse,
Trespassers will be prosecuted.

Sea's over that island,
weed over furrow and dungheap:
but how I should recognise the place
under the weeds and sand
who was never in it on land I dont know:
some trick of refraction,
a film of light in the water crumpled and spread
like a luminous frock on a woman walking
alone in her garden.

Oval face, thin eyebrows wide of the eyes,
a premonition in the gait
of this subaqueous persistence
of a particular year—
for you had prepared it for preservation
not vindictively, urged
by the economy of passions.

Nobody said: She is organising
these knicknacks her dislike collects
into a pattern nature will adopt and perpetuate.

Weed over meadowgrass, sea over weed,
no step on the gravel.
Very likely I shall never meet her again
or if I do, fear the latch as before.

1930

18 THE COMPLAINT OF THE MORPETHSHIRE FARMER

On the up-platform at Morpeth station
in the market-day throng
I overheard a Morpethshire farmer
muttering this song:

Must ye bide, my good stone house,
to keep a townsman dry?
To hear the flurry of the grouse
but not the lowing of the kye?

To see the bracken choke the clod
the coulter will na turn?
The bit level neebody
will drain soak up the burn?

Where are ye, my seven score sheep?
Feeding on other braes!
My brand has faded from your fleece,
another has its place.

The fold beneath the rowan
where ye were dipt before,
its cowpit walls are overgrown,
ye would na heed them more.

And thou! Thou's idled all the spring,
I doubt thou's spoiled, my Meg!
But a sheepdog's faith is aye something.
We'll hire together in Winnipeg.

Canada's a cold land.
Thou and I must share
a straw bed and a hind's wages
and the bitter air.

Canada's a bare land
for the north wind and the snow.
Northumberland's a bare land
for men have made it so.

Sheep and cattle are poor men's food,
grouse is sport for the rich;
heather grows where the sweet grass might grow
for the cost of cleaning the ditch.

A liner lying in the Clyde
will take me to Quebec.
My sons'll see the land I am leaving
as barren as her deck.

1930

19

Fruits breaking the branches,
sunlight stagnates in the rift;
here the curl of a comma,
parenthesis,

(Put the verb out of mind, lurking
to jar all to a period!)
discourse interminably
uncontradicted

level under the orchards'
livid-drowsy green:
this that Elysium
they speak of.

Where shall I hide?

1930

20 VESTIGES

I

Salt grass silent of hooves, the lake stinks,
we take a few small fish from the streams,
our children are scabby, chivvied by flies,
we cannot read the tombs in the eastern prairie,
      who slew the Franks, who
      swam the Yellow River.

The lice have left Temuchin's tent. His ghost
cries under north wind, having spent
strength in life: life lost, lacks means of death,
voice-tost; the horde indistinguishable;
worn name weak in fool's jaws.

We built no temples. Our cities' woven hair
mildewed and frayed. Records of Islam and Chin,
battles, swift riders, ambush,
tale of the slain, and the name Jengiz.

Wild geese of Yen, peacocks of the Windy Shore.

Tall Chutsai sat under the phoenix tree.
—That Baghdad banker contracts to
double the revenue, him collecting.
Four times might be exacted, but
such taxation impoverishes the people.

No litigation. The laws were simple.

II

Jengiz to Chang Chun: China
is fat, but I am lean
eating soldier's food,
lacking learning.
In seven years
I brought most of the world under one law.
The Lords of Cathay
hesitate and fall.
Amidst these disorders
I distrust my talents.
To cross a river
boats and rudders,
to keep the empire in order
poets and sages,
but I have not found nine for a cabinet,
not three.
I have fasted and washed. Come.

Chang: I am old
not wise nor virtuous,
nor likely to be much use.
My appearance is parched, my body weak.
I set out at once.

And to Liu Chung Lu, Jengiz:
Get an escort and a good cart,
and the girls can be sent on
separately if he insists.

1931

21 TWO PHOTOGRAPHS

It's true then that you still overeat, fat friend,
and swell, and never take folk's advice. They laugh,
you just giggle and pay no attention. Damn!
            you dont care, not you!

But once—that was before time had blunted your
desire for pretty frocks—slender girl—or is
the print cunningly faked?—arm in arm with your
            fiancé you stood

and glared into the lens (slightly out of focus)
while that public eye scrutinised your shape,
afraid, the attitude shows, you might somehow
            excite its dislike.

1932

Mesh cast for mackerel
by guess and the sheen's tremor,
imperceptible if you havent the knack—
a difficult job,

hazardous and seasonal:
many shoals all of a sudden,
it would tax the Apostles to take the lot;
then drowse for months,

nets on the shingle,
a pint in the tap.
Likewise the pilchards come unexpectedly,
startle the man on the cliff.

Remember us to the teashop girls.
Say we have seen no legs better than theirs,
we have the sea to stare at,
its treason, copiousness, tedium.

1932

23 THE PASSPORT OFFICER

This impartial dog's nose
scrutinizes the lamppost. All in good order.
He sets his seal on it and
moves on to the next.

(The drippings of his forerunners
convey no information,
barely a precedent.
His actions are reflex.)

1932

Vessels thrown awry by strong gusts
broach to, the seas capsize them.
Sundry cargoes have
strewn the gulf with flotsam
in parcels too small to be salvaged.

(In the purlieus? or the precincts?
Lord Shaw had it argued
a week in the Lords:
a guinea a minute
more or less.)

Some attribute the series of wrecks hereabouts to
faulty stowage, an illfound ship,
careless navigation or the notorious reefs,
just awash at low tide.
The place has a bad name.

(Stern in the purlieus, bow in the precincts,
the mate in the purlieus,
the chief engineer
together with the donkeyman
at that moment in the precincts.)

Nevertheless we have heard
voices speech eludes allude to
gales not measured by the anemometer
nor predicted in Kingsway.
They defy Epicurus.

(Lord Shaw quoted Solomon,
advised a compromise.
Lord Carson muttered
'Purlieus or precincts
the place has a bad name.')

Here was glass-clear architecture,
gardens sacred to Tethys.

Ocean spare the new twinscrew dieselengined tanker,
spare the owners and underwriters
litigation.

1933

25

As appleblossom to crocus
typist to cottage lass,
perishable alike, unlike
the middleclass rose.

Each sour noon
squeezed into teashops
displays one at least
delicate ignorant face

untroubled by
earth's spinning
preoccupied rather
by the set of her stocking.

Men are timid,
hotels expensive,
the police keep
a sharp eye on landladies.

—The cinema, Postume,
Postume, warm,
in the old days
before thirty.

1934

26

Two hundred and seven paces
        from the tram-stop
to the door,

a hundred and forty-six thousand
        four hundred
seconds ago,

two hundred and ninety-two thousand
        eight hundred
kisses or thereabouts; what else

let him say who saw and let
        him who is able
do like it for I'm

not fit for a commonplace world
        any longer, I'm
bound for the City,

cashregister, adding-machine,
        rotary stencil.
Give me another

double whiskey and fire-extinguisher,
        George. Here's
Girls! Girls!

                                        1934

27

On highest summits dawn comes soonest.
(But that is not the time to give over loving.)

1935

28

You leave
nobody else
without a bed

you make
everybody else
thoroughly at home

I'm
the only one
hanged
in your
halter

you've driven
nobody else mad
but me.

1935

Southwind, tell her what
wont sadden her,
not how wretched
I am.

Do you sleep snug these
long nights or
know I am lying
alone?

1935

30 THE OROTAVA ROAD

Four white heifers with sprawling hooves
      trundle the waggon.
    Its ill-roped crates heavy with fruit sway.
The chisel point of the goad, blue and white,
      glitters ahead,
    a flame to follow lance-high in a man's hand
who does not shave. His linen trousers
    like him want washing.
    You can see his baked skin through his shirt.
He has no shoes and his hat has a hole in it.
      'Hu! vaca! Hu! vaca!'
    he says staccato without raising his voice;
'Adios caballero' legato but
      in the same tone.
    Camelmen high on muzzled mounts
boots rattling against the panels
      of an empty
    packsaddle do not answer strangers.

Each with his train of seven or eight tied
                    head to tail they
          pass silent but for the heavy bells
and plip of slobber dripping from
                    muzzle to dust;
          save that on sand their soles squeak slightly.
Milkmaids, friendly girls between
                    fourteen and twenty
          or younger, bolt upright on small
trotting donkeys that bray (they arch their
                    tails a few inches
          from the root, stretch neck and jaw forward
to make the windpipe a trumpet)
                    chatter. Jolted
          cans clatter. The girls' smiles repeat
the black silk curve of the wimple
                    under the chin.
          Their hats are absurd doll's hats
or flat-crowned to take a load.
                    All have fine eyes.
          You can guess their balanced nakedness
under the cotton gown and thin shift.
                    They sing and laugh.
          They say 'Adios!' shyly but look back
more than once, knowing our thoughts
                    and sharing our
          desires and lack of faith in desire.

                                        1935

O ubi campi!

The soil sandy and the plow light, neither
virgin land nor near by the market town,
cropping one staple without forethought, steer
stedfastly ruinward year in year out,
grudging the labour and cost of manure,
drudging not for gain but fewer dollars loss
yet certain to make a bad bargain by
misjudging the run of prices. How glad
you will be when the state takes your farm for
arrears of taxes! No more cold daybreaks
saffron under the barbed wire the east wind
thrums, nor wet noons, nor starpinned nights! The choir
of gnats is near a full-close. The windward
copse stops muttering inwardly its prose
bucolics. You will find a city job
or relief—or doss-and-grub—resigned to
anything except your own numb toil, the
seasonal plod to spoil the land, alone.

1936

Let them remember Samangan, the bridge and tower
and rutted cobbles and the coppersmith's hammer,
where we looked out from the walls to the marble mountains,
ate and lay and were happy an hour and a night;

so that the heart never rests from love of the city
without lies or riches, whose old women
straight as girls at the well are beautiful,
its old men and its wineshops gay.

Let them remember Samangan against usurers,
cheats and cheapjacks, amongst boasters,
hideous children of cautious marriages,
those who drink in contempt of joy.

Let them remember Samangan, remember
they wept to remember the hour and go.

1937

33

To Anne de Silver

I

Not to thank dogwood nor
the wind that sifts
petals are these words,
nor for a record,

but, as notes sung and received
still the air,
these are controlled by
yesterday evening,

a peal after
the bells have rested.

II

Lest its meaning
escape the dogwood's
whiteness, these:

Days now
less bitter than
rind of wild gourd.
Cool breezes. Lips
moistened, there are words.

1938

34

To Violet, with prewar poems

These tracings from a world that's dead
take for my dust-smothered pyramid.
Count the sharp study and long toil
as pavements laid for worms to soil.
You without knowing it might tread
the grass where my foundation's laid,
your, or another's, house be built
where my weathered stones lie spilt,
and this unread memento be
the only lasting part of me.

1941

35

Search under every veil
for the pale eyes, pale
lips of a sick child,
in each doorway glimpse
her reluctant limbs
for whom no kindness is,
to whom caress and kiss
come nightly more amiss,
whose hand no gentle hand
touches, whose eyes withstand
compassion. Say: Done, past
help, preordained waste.
Say: We know by the dead
they mourn, their bloodshed,
the maimed who are the free.
We willed it, we.
Say: Who am I to doubt?
But every vein cries out.

1947

36

See! Their verses are laid
as mosaic gold to gold
gold to lapis lazuli
white marble to porphyry
stone shouldering stone, the dice
polished alike, there is
no cement seen and no gap
between stones as the frieze strides
to the impending apse:
the rays of many glories
forced to its focus forming
a glory neither of stone
nor metal, neither of words
nor verses, but of the light
shining upon no substance;
a glory not made
for which all else was made.

1948

37 ON THE FLY-LEAF OF POUND'S CANTOS

There are the Alps. What is there to say about them?
They don't make sense. Fatal glaciers, crags cranks climb,
jumbled boulder and weed, pasture and boulder, scree,
et l'on entend, maybe, *le refrain joyeux et leger.*
Who knows what the ice will have scraped on the rock it is
smoothing?

There they are, you will have to go a long way round
if you want to avoid them.
It takes some getting used to. There are the Alps,
fools! Sit down and wait for them to crumble!

1949

SECOND BOOK OF ODES

A thrush in the syringa sings.

'Hunger ruffles my wings, fear,
lust, familiar things.

Death thrusts hard. My sons
by hawk's beak, by stones,
trusting weak wings
by cat and weasel, die.

Thunder smothers the sky.
From a shaken bush I
list familiar things,
fear, hunger, lust.'

O gay thrush!

1964

2

Three Michaelmas daisies
on an ashtray;
one abets love;
one droops and woos;

one stiffens her petals
remembering
the root, the sap
and the bees' play.

1965

3 BIRTHDAY GREETING

Gone to hunt; and my brothers,
but the hut is clean, said the girl.
I have curds, besides whey.

Pomegranates, traveller;
butter, if you need it,
in a bundle of cress.

Soft, so soft, my bed.
Few come this road.
I am not married:—yet

today I am fourteen years old.

1965

4

You idiot! What makes you think decay will
never stink from your skin? Your warts sicken
typists, girls in the tube avoid you. Must they
also stop their ears to your tomcat
wailing, a promise your body cannot keep?

A lame stag, limping after the hinds, with tines
shivered by impact and scarred neck—but
look! Spittle fills his mouth, overflows,
snuffing their sweet scent. His feet lift lightly
with mere memory of gentler seasons. Lungs
full of the drug, antlers rake back, he
halts the herd, his voice filled with
custom of combat and unslaked lust.

Did the girl shrink from David? Did she hug his
ribs, death shaking them, and milk dry
the slack teat from which Judah had sucked life?

1965

5

Under sand clay. Dig, wait.
Billy half full, none for the car.
Quartz, salt in well wall,
ice refract first ray.
Canvas udders sag, drip,
swell without splash the mirage
between islands. Knee-deep
camels, lean men, flap-dugged
matrons and surly children.

Aneiza, kin to the
unawed dynast haggling with God.
This brine slaked him as
this sun shrinks.

1965

6 WHAT THE CHAIRMAN TOLD TOM

Poetry? It's a hobby.
I run model trains.
Mr Shaw there breeds pigeons.

It's not work. You dont sweat.
Nobody pays for it.
You *could* advertise soap.

Art, that's opera; or repertory—
The Desert Song.
Nancy was in the chorus.

But to ask for twelve pounds a week—
married, aren't you?—
you've got a nerve.

How could I look a bus conductor
in the face
if I paid you twelve pounds?

Who says it's poetry, anyhow?
My ten year old
can do it *and* rhyme.

I get three thousand and expenses,
a car, vouchers,
but I'm an accountant.

They do what I tell them,
my company.
What do *you* do?

Nasty little words, nasty long words,
it's unhealthy.
I want to wash when I meet a poet.

They're Reds, addicts,
all delinquents.
What you write is rot.

Mr Hines says so, and he's a schoolteacher,
he ought to know.
Go and find *work*.

1965

7

Ille mi par esse deo videtur

O, it is godlike to sit selfpossessed
when her chin rises and she turns to smile;
but my tongue thickens, my ears ring,
what I see is hazy.

I tremble. Walls sink in night, voices
unmeaning as wind. She only
a clear note, dazzle of light, fills
furlongs and hours

so that my limbs stir without will, lame,
I a ghost, powerless,
treading air, drowning, sucked
back into dark

unless, rafted on light or music,
drawn into her radiance, I dissolve
when her chin rises and she turns to smile.
O, it is godlike!

1965

8

Carmencita's tawny paps
glow through a threadbare frock;
stance bold, and her look.
Filth guards her chastity,
              Ay de mi chica!

Lips salty, her hair
matted, powdered with ash;
sweat sublimes from her armpit
when the young men go past

seeking silk and elaborate
manners and strange scent.
She turns to sigh,
lifting her hem to pick a louse from her thigh.
              Ay de mi muchachita!

                                        1965

9

All the cants they peddle
bellow entangled,
teeth for knots and
each other's ankles,
to become stipendiary
in any wallow;
crow or weasel
each to his fellow.

Yet even these,
even these might
listen as crags
listen to light
and pause, uncertain
of the next beat,
each dancer alone
with his foolhardy feet.

1969

Stones trip Coquet burn;
grass trails, tickles
till her glass thrills.

The breeze she wears
lifts and falls back.
Where beast cool

in midgy shimmer
she dares me chase
under a bridge,

giggles, ceramic
huddle of notes,
darts from gorse

and I follow, fooled.
She must rest, surely;
some steep pool

to plodge or dip
and silent taste
with all my skin.

1970

At Briggflatts meetinghouse

Boasts time mocks cumber Rome. Wren
set up his own monument.
Others watch fells dwindle, think
the sun's fires sink.

Stones indeed sift to sand, oak
blends with saints' bones.
Yet for a little longer here
stone and oak shelter

silence while we ask nothing
but silence. Look how clouds dance
under the wind's wing, and leaves
delight in transience.

1975

Perche no spero

Now we've no hope of going back,
cutter, to that grey quay
where we moored twice and twice unwillingly
cast off our cables to put out at the slack
when the sea's laugh was choked to a mutter
and the leach lifted hesitantly with a stutter
and sulky clack,

how desolate the swatchways look,
cutter, and the chart's stained,
stiff, old, wrinkled and uncertain,
seeming to contradict the pilot book.
On naked banks a few birds strut
to watch the ebb sluice through a narrowing gut
loud as a brook.

Soon, while that northwest squall wrings out its cloud,
cutter, we'll heave to
free of the sands and let the half moon do
as it pleases, hanging there in the port shrouds
like a riding light. We have no course to set,
only to drift too long, watch too glumly, and wait,
wait.

1980

OVERDRAFTS

Darling of Gods and Men, beneath the gliding stars
you fill rich earth and buoyant sea with your presence
for every living thing achieves its life through you,
rises and sees the sun. For you the sky is clear,
the tempests still. Deft earth scatters her gentle flowers,
the level ocean laughs, the softened heavens glow
with generous light for you. In the first days of spring
when the untrammelled allrenewing southwind blows
the birds exult in you and herald your coming.
Then the shy cattle leap and swim the brooks for love.
Everywhere, through all seas mountains and waterfalls,
love caresses all hearts and kindles all creatures
to overmastering lust and ordained renewals.
Therefore, since you alone control the sum of things
and nothing without you comes forth into the light
and nothing beautiful or glorious can be
without you, Alma Venus! trim my poetry
with your grace; and give peace to write and read and think.

(Lucretius)

1927

Yes, it's slow, docked of amours,
      docked of the doubtless efficacious
bottled makeshift, gin; but who'd risk being bored stiff
every night listening to father's silly sarcasms?

If your workbox is mislaid
      blame Cytherea's lad . . . Minerva
's not at all pleased that your seam's dropped for a fair sight
of that goodlooking athlete's glistening wet shoulders

when he's been swimming and stands
      towelling himself in full view
of the house. Ah! but you should see him on horseback!
or in track-shorts! He's a first-class middleweight pug.

He can shoot straight from the butts,
      straight from precarious cover, waistdeep
in the damp sedge, having stayed motionless daylong
when the driven tiger appears suddenly at arms'-length.

(Horace)

1931

Please stop gushing about his pink
neck smooth arms and so forth, Dulcie; it makes me sick,
badtempered, silly: makes me blush.
Dribbling sweat on my chops proves I'm on tenterhooks.
—White skin bruised in a boozing bout,
ungovernable cub certain to bite out a
permanent memorandum on
those lips. Take my advice, better not count on your
tough guy's mumbling your pretty mouth
always. Only the thrice blest are in love for life,
we others are divorced at heart
soon, soon torn apart by wretched bickerings.

(Horace)

1931

VERSE AND VERSION

In that this happening
          is not unkind
it put to
          shame every kindness

mind, mouths, their words,
          people, put sorrow
               on
          its body

before sorrow it came
          and before every kindness,
happening for every sorrow
          before every kindness

(Louis Zukofsky)

quia id quod accidit
          non est immitis
pudebat omnia
          mitiora.

mens, ora, dicta horum,
          hominesque, tristitiam
superimponunt
          eius membra.

prius quam tristitia accidit,
          omnisque prius quam mitiora;
accidit pro omnibus tristitiis
          prius quam omnia mitiora.

(Basil Bunting)

1932

Once, so they say, pinetrees seeded on Pelion's peak swam
over the clear sea waves to the surf on the beaches of Phasis
when the gamesome fleece-filchers, pith of Argos, picked for a foray,
bearded the surge in a nimble ship, deal sweeps swirling the waters.
The Lady of Citadels shaped them a light hull for darting to windward
and laid the cutaway keel with her own hands and wedded the timbers.
That ship first daunted untamed Amphitrite. When her forefoot
scattered the fickle calm and oarwrenched waves kindled with spindrift
the mermaids rose from the dazzling sluices of the sound to gaze at the
marvel.
Then, ah then! mortal eyes, and by day, had sight of the sea-girls
and marked their naked bodies stretched breasthigh out of the tiderace.
Forthwith, thus the tale runs, love of Thetis flamed up in Peleus
and Thetis took Peleus spite of the briefness of man's lifetime;
even her father himself deemed Peleus worthy of Thetis.

Health to you, heroes, brood of the gods, born in the prime season,
thoroughbreds sprung of thoroughbred dams, health to you aye, and
again health!
I will talk to you often in my songs, but first I speak to you, bridegroom
acclaimed with many pinebrands, pillar of Thessaly, fool for luck, Peleus,
to whom Jove the godbegetter, Jove himself yielded his mistress,
for the sea's own child clung to you

—*and why Catullus bothered to write pages and pages of this drivel mystifies
me.*

1933

When the sword of sixty comes nigh his head
give a man no wine, for he is drunk with years.
Age claps a stick in my bridle-hand:
substance spent, health broken,
forgotten the skill to swerve aside from the joust
with the spearhead grazing my eyelashes.

The sentinel perched on the hill top
cannot see the countless army he used to see there:
the black summit's deep in snow
and its lord himself sinning against the army.

He was proud of his two swift couriers:
lo! sixty ruffians have put them in chains.
The singer is weary of his broken voice,
one drone for the bulbul alike and the lion's grousing.

Alas for flowery, musky, sappy thirty
and the sharp Persian sword!
The pheasant strutting about the briar,
pomegranate-blossom and cypress sprig!
Since I raised my glass to fifty-eight
I have toasted only the bier and the burial ground.

I ask the just Creator
so much refuge from Time
that a tale of mine may remain in the world
from this famous book of the ancients
and they who speak of such matters weighing their words
think of that only when they think of me.

(Firdosi)

1935

136

Abu'abdulla Ja'far bin Mahmud Rudaki of Samarkand says:

All the teeth ever I had are worn down and fallen out.
They were not rotten teeth, they shone like a lamp,
a row of silvery-white pearls set in coral;
they were as the morning star and as drops of rain.
There are none left now, all of them wore out and fell out.
Was it ill-luck, ill-luck, a malign conjunction?
It was no fault of stars, nor yet length of years.
I will tell you what it was: it was God's decree.

The world is always like a round, rolling eye,
round and rolling since it existed: a cure for pain
and then again a pain that supplants the cure.
In a certain time it makes new things old,
in a certain time makes new what was worn threadbare.
Many a broken desert has been gay garden,
many gay gardens grow where there used to be desert.

What can you know, my blackhaired beauty,
what I was like in the old days?
You tickle your lover with your curls
but never knew the time when he had curls.
The days are past when his face was good to look on,
the days are past when his hair was jet black.
Likewise, comeliness of guests and friends was dear,
but one dear guest will never return.
Many a beauty may you have marvelled at
but I was always marvelling at her beauty.
The days are past when she was glad and gay
and overflowing with mirth and I was afraid of losing her.
He paid, your lover, well and in counted coin
in any town where was a girl with round hard breasts,
and plenty of good girls had a fancy for him
and came by night but by day dare not
for dread of the husband and the jail.

Bright wine and the sight of a gracious face,
dear it might cost, but always cheap to me.
My purse was my heart, my heart bursting with words,
and the title-page of my book was Love and Poetry.
Happy was I, not understanding grief,

any more than a meadow.
Silk-soft has poetry made many a heart
stone before and heavy as an anvil.

Eyes turned always towards little nimble curls,
ears turned always towards men wise in words,
neither household, wife, child nor a patron—
at ease of these trials and at rest!
Oh! my dear, you look at Rudaki
but never saw him in the days when he was like that.

Never saw him when he used to go about
singing his songs as though he had a thousand.
The days are past when bold men sought his company,
the days are past when he managed affairs of princes,
the days are past when all wrote down his verses,
the days are past when he was the Poet of Khorassan.

Wherever there was a gentleman of renown
in his house had I silver and a mount.
From whomsoever some had greatness and gifts,
greatness and gifts had I from the house of Saman.
The Prince of Khorassan gave me forty thousand dirhems,
Prince Makan more by a fifth,
and eight thousand in all from his nobles
severally. That was the fine time!
When the Prince heard a fair phrase he gave, and his men,
each man of his nobles, as much as the Prince saw fit.
Times have changed. I have changed. Bring me my stick.
Now for the beggar's staff and wallet.

(Rudaki)

1948

Shall I sulk because my love has a double heart?
Happy is he whose she is singlehearted!
She has found me a new torment for every instant
and I am, whatever she does, content, content.
If she has bleached my cheek with her love, say: Bleach!
Is not pale saffron prized above poppy red?
If she has stooped my shoulders, say to them: Stoop!
Must not a harp be bent when they string it to sing?
If she has kindled fire in my heart, say: Kindle!
Only a kindled candle sends forth light.
If tears rain from my eyes, say: Let them rain!
Spring rains make fair gardens. And if then
she has cast me into the shadow of exile, say:
Those who seek fortune afar find it the first.

(from a qasida of Manuchehri)

1949

Came to me—
      Who?
She.
      When?
In the dawn, afraid.

      What of?
Anger.
      Whose?
Her father's.
      Confide!

I kissed her twice.
      Where?
On her moist mouth.
      Mouth?

No.
      What, then?
Cornelian.
      How was it?
Sweet.

(Rudaki)

1949

This I write, mix ink with tears,
and have written of grief before, but never so grievously,
to tell Azra Vamiq's pain,
to tell Laila Majnun's plight,
to tell you my own
unfinished story.
Take it. Seek no excuse.
How sweetly you will sing what I so sadly write.

(attributed, probably wrongly, to Sa'di)

1949

Last night without sight of you my brain was ablaze.
My tears trickled and fell plip on the ground. That I with
sighing might bring my life to a close they would name
you and again and again speak your name till
with night's coming all eyes closed save mine whose every
hair pierced my scalp like a lancet. That was
not wine I drank far from your sight but my heart's
blood gushing into the cup. Wall and door wherever
I turned my eyes scored and decorated with shapes
of you. To dream of Laila Majnun prayed for
sleep. My senses came and went but neither your
face saw I nor would your fantom go from me.
Now like aloes my heart burned, now smoked as a censer.
Where was the morning gone that used on other nights
to breathe till the horizon paled? Sa'di!
Has then the chain of the Pleiades broken
tonight that every night is hung on the sky's neck?

(Sa'di)

1949

You can't grip years, Postume,
that ripple away nor hold back
wrinkles and, soon now, age,
nor can you tame death

not if you paid three hundred
bulls every day that goes by
to Pluto, who has no tears,
who has dyked up

giants where we'll go aboard,
we who feed on the soil,
to cross, kings some, some
penniless plowmen.

For nothing we keep out of war
or from screaming spindrift
or wrap ourselves against autumn,
for nothing, seeing

we must stare at that dark, slow
drift and watch the damned
toil, while all they build
tumbles back on them.

We must let earth go and home,
wives too, and your trim trees,
yours for a moment, save one
sprig of black cypress.

Better men will empty
bottles we locked away,
wine puddle our table,
fit wine for a pope.

(Horace)

1971

HOW DUKE VALENTINE CONTRIVED

(*the murder of Vitellozzo Vitelli, Oliverotto da Fermo, Mr.
Pagolo and the Duke of Gravina Orsini*) *according to*
Machiavelli:

Duke Valentine had been in Lombardy with the King
clearing up the slanders the Florentines had put about
concerning the rising at Arezzo and in Val di Chiana,
and lay in Imola scheming
        how to keep his men occupied,
        how to turn John Bentivoglia
        out of Bologna, a
        city he coveted
        to make his capital there.
        The Vitelli heard of it
and the Orsini and the rest of the gang
and it was more than they would put up with
        for they supposed
it would be their turn next
one by one.
So they held a diet and asked the Cardinal,
Pagolo,
Gravina Orsini, Vitellozzo Vitelli, Oliverotto da Fermo,
John Paul Baglioni tyrant of Perugia,
and Mister Anthony of Venafro
representing Pandolfo Petruccio boss of Siena,
and discussed the Duke's intentions,
estimated his strength,
and said it was time to put a stop to it.
Resolved:
        not to let Bentivoglia down
        and to get the Florentines
        on their side.
        So they sent fellows
to hearten the one and persuade the other.

As soon as the news got about the malcontents took heart
throughout the Duke's territory. Some from Urbino
went out against a fortress held by the Duke's troops

who were busy hauling timber to mend their stockade
and certain beams were lying on the drawbridge
        so they couldnt raise it
        so the conspirators
hopped up onto the bridge and thence into the fortress:
upon which the whole province rebelled
and sent for their old duke,
trusting the lords of the diet to see them through,
and sent them word; and *they* thought
they oughtnt to let a chance like that slip,
        collected an army
        and marched at once
        to reduce the strongholds.

Meanwhile they sent to Florence a second time,
'the game was won already and such a chance
not likely to happen again,' but the Florentines
loathed
both the Vitelli and Orsini for various reasons
and sent Niccolo Machiavelli to the Duke instead
        to offer help.
He found him in Imola, scared at the turn of events,
        just what he hadnt expected
        happening all of a sudden,
        his soldiers disaffected,
        disarmed, so to speak,
and a war on his hands. But he cheered up
and thought he might stave things off
with a few men and a lot of negotiations
until he could raise a reliable army.

        He borrowed men from the King
        and hired a few himself
        men at arms or
anybody who knew how to manage a horse.
        He even paid them.

        All the same
his enemies came to Fossombrone
where some of his men were gathered and scattered them,
so he had to negotiate for all he was worth
        (and he was a first rate humbug).

145

It seems 'they were taking by force
              what they might have as a gift
for the title was all that he wanted,
              let them do the ruling.'
Whereupon they suspended hostilities
              and sent Mr. Pagolo
to draw up an armistice: but the Duke
              kept on recruiting
              men and remounts,
sending them into Romagna to be less conspicuous.

When five hundred French lancers arrived
              he was strong enough to fight
but thought it safer and more sensible, on the whole,
              to cozen his enemies,
and worked it so that they signed a treaty
getting back their former powers
with four thousand ducats indemnity,
and he promised to let Bentivoglia alone
and marry into the family: and they,
to hand over Urbino and other occupied places,
              not to make war without his consent,
              not to take jobs in other armies.

Duke Guidobaldo had to clear out of Urbino
and go back to Venice, but first
he had all the forts pulled down
for as he judged
the people were on his side and how was another to rule them
without forts? Duke Valentine
sent the rest of his men into Romagna
and went to Cesena about the end of November
where he spent several days discussing what was next to be done
with envoys from the Vitelli and Orsini
who were with their armies in Urbino,
but nothing came of it till they sent Oliverotto
and 'they would deal with Tuscany if he liked,
or if that wouldnt do, should they go take Sinigaglia?'
He replied he was friends with the Florentines
              but Sinigaglia
              would suit him nicely.

A few days later
they sent to him that the town had surrendered
but the citadel
would not surrender unless to the Duke in person,
would he please come?
It seemed a good opportunity
and there could be no offence
in going by invitation,
so to put them off their guard
he sent away the French troops,
back into Lombardy except a hundred lancers
under the Right Reverend Ciandeles, his brother-in-law,
and left Cesena about the middle of December
for Fano where, as craftily as he knew how,
he set about persuading the Vitelli and Orsini
to wait for him in Sinigaglia, pointing out
unneighbourliness did not make for a durable peace,
whereas he was a man who could and would appreciate
his allies' arms and advice. Vitellozzo
was uneasy, he had learned from his brother's death
not to trust a prince he had once offended,
but Orsini argued
and the Duke sent presents
and rotten promises
till he consented.
The night before (that was December the thirtieth
fifteen hundred and two)—the night before
he was leaving Fano the Duke explained his plan
to eight men he thought he could trust,
amongst them the Reverend Michael
and d'Euna, the Right Reverend,
afterwards Cardinal: and charged them,
when Vitellozzo, Pagolo Orsino,
the Duke of Gravina and Oliverotto
should come out to meet him,
a couple to each of them,
these two to this one,
those two to that one,
should ride beside them
and make conversation
right into Sinigaglia and not lose sight of them
until they should come to his lodging and be taken.

147

He ordered all the troops,
more than two thousand horse,
ten thousand foot,
to be ready at daybreak on the Metaurus' banks,
a river five miles from Fano,
and on the last of December
joined them there and sent five hundred horse ahead,
then all the infantry, and after them
he himself with the rest of the men-at-arms.

Fano and Sinigaglia are towns of the Marches
fifteen miles apart on the Adriatic.
Going to Sinigaglia you have the mountains on your right,
very close to the sea in some places,
nowhere two miles away.
Sinigaglia city
stands about a bow-shot from the foot of the mountains
less than a mile from the shore. A little stream runs by it
wetting the wall towards Fano. When the road
is nearing Sinigaglia it skirts the mountains,
turns left, follows the stream,
and crosses by a bridge nearly opposite the gate
which is at right angles to the wall. Between it and the bridge
there is a suburb with a square, and a bend of the stream
bounds it on two sides.

Since the Vitelli and Orsini
had made up their minds
to wait for the Duke
and do the handsome thing
they had sent their soldiers out of Sinigaglia
to a castle six miles away to make room for the Duke's troops.
There were none left in the town but Liverotto's lot,
a thousand infantry and a hundred and fifty horse,
who were billetted in the suburb. This was how things stood
while Duke Valentine was on his way to Sinigaglia.

When the advance guard came to the bridge
they did not cross
but formed up on either side of the road in two files
and the infantry went between and halted inside the town.
Vitellozzo, Pagolo, and the Duke of Gravina

took mules and went to meet the Duke
with a small mounted escort; and Vitellozzo,
unarmed, in a tunic with green facings,
as glum as though he knew what was going to happen,
was
(considering his courage and the luck he had had in the past)
          rather admirable. They say when he quit his people
to come and meet the Duke at Sinigaglia
he took a sort of last farewell,
bid the captains look after his family,
and admonished his nephews not to rely on the clan's luck
but remember their father's and uncle's valour.

These three came to the Duke and greeted him politely.
He received them smiling; and immediately
those whose task it was were about them.
But Liverotto
was waiting in Sinigaglia with his men
on the square outside his billets by the river,
drilling them to keep them out of mischief.
The Duke noticed, and tipped a wink to the Rev. Michael
who was responsible for Liverotto. Michael rode ahead
and 'it was imprudent to keep his men out of their billets
since the Duke's troopers were sure to occupy them
if found empty. Let him dismiss the parade
and come with him to the Duke.'
When the Duke saw him he called out
and Liverotto saluted and joined the others.

They rode into Sinigaglia,
          dismounted at the Duke's lodgings
and went with him into an inner room,
          and there they were taken;
and the Duke got straight back on horseback and ordered his
                                        scallawags
to pillage Liverotto's men and the Orsini's.
Liverotto's were handy and were pillaged.
          The Orsini's and Vitelli's
          some distance away,
          having had wind of the matter,
          had time to prepare.

149

They got away
in close order
with the Vitelli's traditional courage and discipline
in spite of hostile inhabitants and armed enemies.
The Duke's soldiers
were not satisfied with plundering Liverotto's men
and began to sack Sinigaglia, and if he hadnt
checked their insolence by hanging a lot of them
they would have finished the job.

Night fell, the rioting abated,
and the Duke thought it opportune
to put an end to Vitellozzo and Liverotto,
and had them led out to a suitable place and strangled.
Neither said anything worthy of the occasion,
for Vitellozzo begged them to ask of the Pope
a plenary indulgence for his sins,
while Liverotto was blubbering
and putting all the blame for their treason on Vitellozzo.

Pagolo and the Duke of Gravina Orsini
were left alive until the Pope sent word
he had taken Cardinal Orsino, Archbishop of Florence,
together with Mr. James da Santa Croce:
upon which, on the eighteenth of January, at Castel della Pieve,
they were strangled in the same manner.

1933

THE PIOUS CAT

THE PIOUS CAT

by Obaid-e Zakani (and Basil Bunting)

By your leave!

Sagacious and circumspect persons, attend!
This is a story of cats and mice,
how constantly they quarrel and contend.
It is short, truthful and precise.
Listen sharply. Do not miss a minute,
there is so much meaning and deep wisdom in it,
and learned science and politic guile
and rime and rhetoric and style.

By Heaven's decree there was a cat
in Haltwhistle, rough, rich and fat.
His fur was like a coat of mail
with lion's claws and leopard's tail.
When he went out and wailed at night
he made policemen shake with fright.
When he crouched in a flowerbed
big game hunters turned pale with dread.
All creatures beside him seemed tame.
Tibbald was this hero's name.

One day he visited the cellar
to scout for mice. Behind a pillar
he lay in ambush like a bandit
and it fell out as he had planned it—
a mouse crept from a crack and squeaked,
then leapt on a cask of beer (that leaked)
to drink, and shortly drank again.
Beer made him truculent and vain.
He snapped his fingers. 'Where's the cat?
I'll make his skin into a doormat.
I'll teach him: I'll give him what-for.
Cats? One good mouse can lick a score!
Tibbald! Who's he? Let him sneer and purr,
he'll cringe to me. The cat's a cur!'

Tibbald kept mum, but in the pause
you could hear him sharpening his teeth and claws.
When they were keen he made one jump
and caught the drunken mouse by the rump.

Mouse said: 'Please mister, let me off!
I did not mean to boast and scoff.
What I said was said in liquor,
and tipsy tongues talk ten times quicker
than sober sense. Dont bear a grudge!'
but Tibbald only answered: 'Fudge!
Bring your remarks to a fullstop,'
then ate him and lapped the gravy up.

Next Tibbald went to the wash basin
he used to scrub his hands and face in,
and brushed his tail and combed his hair
and went to church and said this prayer:

'Lord, I confess the awful vice
of breakfasting on little mice;
but, Father, I repent sincerely.
I will pay—not a pittance merely
but more than ample compensation.
To every surviving relation
or legal representative
of my poor victim, I will give . . .
some cold coffee and plenty of tea
(on proper proof of identity,
birth certificate and passport
and other documents of that sort);
and I will gobble no more mice
in stews or sausages or pies
nor *table d'hôte* nor *à la carte*.
An humble and a contrite heart
thinks lettuces and things like that
as sweet as a tender farmyard rat.'
Here his repentance went so deep
that Tibbald could not choose but weep.

A mouse had hidden behind the pulpit.
He heard Tib's sob and watched him gulp it,
then ran all the way home and blurted:
'Good news! the cat has been converted!
He has turned charitable and meek
and means to fast six days a week,
and on the seventh he will eat
acorns and trash instead of mouse-meat.'
So all the mice cried: 'Halleluia!
You dont suppose he'll relapse though, do ye?'

To give their gratitude a vent
seven eminent mice were sent
to take Saint Tibbald a testimonial.
They marched with dignified ceremonial
and every mouse of them had brought
gifts of the most expensive sort.
The first mouse brought a bottle of Schiedam.
The second brought a roast leg of lamb.
The third mouse brought a red currant tart;
the fourth, spaghetti by the yard;
the fifth, hot dogs with Cocacola.
The sixth brought bread and gorgonzola.
The seventh mouse brought a homemade
plumcake and a jug of lemonade.
Their manners were courteous and wellbred.
They bowed respectfully and said:
'Long live the cat! May we enquire,
is your health all you can desire?
Deign to accept this trifling token
of compliments we will leave unspoken.'

'Upon my word' said Tib, 'here's dinner!
Since breakfast, I have got much thinner
by fasting. Service and self denial
were evidently worth the trial
since Just and Merciful Providence
sends me the Reward of Abstinence.
It sees my worth (Who can deny it?)
and furnishes me a richer diet.

I am sure a good conscience always led
to a larger share of Daily Bread.
Dear friends! Kind comrades! Fellow creatures!
Come nearer. Let me see your features.'

The mice were flustered and in a dither
but they stepped forward all together
until they came within arm's length.
Then Tibbald suddenly showed his strength
and skill, and in a little moment
they found out what fair words from a foe meant,
for two to left and two to right
and one between his jaws to bite
(that makes five) he caught in so cunning a way
that only two were saved by running away.

'Woe and disaster! Fellow mice,
can you stand by and watch your neighbours
guzzled before your very eyes?
Quick, oil your rifles, whet your sabres.
This foul aggression must be fought out.'
Then all the mice cried: 'Shame and pity!
Refer the facts to a committee
and while they are getting a report out
we'll have our mourning made to order,
hem handkerchiefs with a black border
to wipe our turbulent tears away
with due and dignified delay
until they tell us the King of Mice is
ready to meet this urgent crisis.'

The king was grave and proud and prim.
They brought him the report to skim.
The gist and pith of it was that:
'Oh King, consider the cruel cat.
Once on a time that ravenous ratter ate
his daily mouse at a steady flat rate
but since he took to prayers and pieties
he bolts us down by whole societies.'

On this, His Majesty undertook
to bring the criminal cat to book
and signed a royal proclamation
to mobilize the entire nation
with rifles, bayonets, pistols, shells,
swords, gasmasks and whatever else
might come in handy on a campaign,
such as antidotes against rat-bane.

His general held a grand parade
where twenty regiments displayed
smart uniforms of every shade.
Their caps were stiff, their buttons bright,
belts and boots polished, blouses tight,
hair cut, trousers pressed, webbing white,
and ribbons blazed on every bust.
The swaggering general staff discussed:
'What are our war aims? How shall we state 'em?
What must we put in our ultimatum?
Breach of treaty? Gross atrocity?'
but when they had whittled away their verbosity
the king's ambassador, grave and sly,
carried this message: 'Submit or die.'

Now stop your ears, maid, matron, bride!
Switch off your hearing aids and hide
your faces in your wraps and shawls,
for Tibbald answered roughly: '⌗'.
But when he had watched the messenger mount, he
called all the cats he could find in the county
and drilled them daily on the fells
to scratch, bite, and fire off rockets and shells
till one cold dawn they saw the host
of mice advancing from the coast.

Grim was the onslaught! Dead and dying
lay close as chipped potatoes frying,
with hiss, roar, groan and bubble.
Arms, legs, tails, whiskers strewed the moor
like muck spread thick on winter stubble.

⌗ a word in cattish language meaning 'Oh dear me, *what* nonsense!'

A million dead? No, no! Far more.
When Tibbald charged with his best equipped
storm troops, near mouse H.Q. he slipped
and wallowed in the mud. In a trice
he was tied up by nearly a hundred mice.
'Victory' the victors cried.
'Now this war criminal must be tried.'

The warrant was drawn under the king's signet. He
called on the judges for speed and dignity,
so as they assembled to try the crime
they slapped on their black caps to save time,
then sentenced him with solemn squeals
to be hung by the neck and then by the heels.
Fast workmen got the gallows built
while the Bench established Tibbald's guilt.

But while the High Tribunal tried him
the cat was gnawing the thongs that tied him
till with a resolute wrench he bust his
bonds and swallowed the Lord Chief Justice.
King, heroes, hangman, all the hamper,
I wish you could have seen them scamper.

That's where this story comes to a stop.
Now, if you think I made it up
you're wrong. I never. It wasnt me,
it was Obaid-e Zakani.

UNCOLLECTED POEMS

EDITOR'S PREFACE

Bunting collected his own poems. The canon which he established in 1968 he maintained, with few alterations or additions, up to the year of his death, when he released a single poem for inclusion in *Collected Poems*, the body of work which forms the first section of this book. This section does not pretend to alter that.

Uncollected Poems draws together pieces of Bunting's poetry which exist outside that canon: pieces which he at some stage treated as finished, and either published, or intended to publish, or allowed others to publish, or circulated, or simply didn't destroy (he was an expert with fireplace and waste bin). The slight disservice to scholars, who enjoy rummaging in obscure places after fugitive items, may be offset by the convenience of having the work in one volume.

Yet critics will say that Bunting would have preferred the work to remain uncollected (Ode I: 11 states their case) and to be sure he did not wish to collect the poems, or have them collected, *in his lifetime*. But he cooperated with those who did collect them (notably Roger Guedalla, whose bibliography provides the source in many cases) and sanctioned their recirculation (for instance, in Sister Victoria Forde's thesis, and in the festschrift for Jonathan Williams): he was fully aware of the interest they would excite, and never blind to the likelihood of their resurrection. All the work herein is easy to trace in one way or another, if not readily accessible: it is necessary to present it in order to define it, and distinguish it from *Collected Poems*.

In the case of a lesser writer, this would be work of largely surgical interest. I confess freely to having enjoyed the task: Bunting's fugitive pieces, though undeniably uneven, are never without quality, and are often of the highest order. 'They Say Etna' and 'Hymn to alias Thor', Pound-pastiche as they are, still read well, and it would be hard to argue the case for continuing to restrict access to work from Bunting's remarkable post-'Briggflatts' period such as 'Such syllables flicker . . .'(Uncollected Ode 11), or the brief epitaph for Lorine Niedecker (Uncollected Ode 10).

Some of these poems made their way, in edited versions, into *Collected Poems*: the differences are instructive. Otherwise, I have excluded all rough and early versions, uncirculated fragments, and all pieces of dubious ascription (including poems copied by others from notes which Bunting subsequently destroyed). If others can spot glaring oversights in what remains, to some extent, the precursor of a (distant) full scholarly edition, I hope they will tell me of them. Such other comment as is necessary I have included in my notes, along with citations and sources.

Where variant texts exist I have, with very few exceptions, chosen what appears to be the latest, or more complete version. I have maintained Bunting's orthography, punctuation and capitalization with only a few minor exceptions where obvious errors would irritate the reader, or where house style prevailed. In upholding Bunting's preferred textual arrangement (Longer poems: Odes: Overdrafts) I have been faced with difficult decisions (is his Baudelaire too free to be regarded as a translation? should not 'Trinacria' be an overdraft? etc.): I hope my final choices are sufficiently justified to require no further apology. Chronology within each section is never more than approximate. In short, the intention has been to create a readable supplement to *Collected Poems*.

RC (1993)

THEY SAY ETNA

THEY SAY ETNA

They say Etna
belches as much poison
as Duisburg's pudenda
a littering sow
helpless in the railroad ditch.

                    Gear and gear.

The Muses Ergot and Appiol,
                              Mr Reader.
Mr Reader,
              the Muses Ergot and Appiol.
What violence or fraud
shall we record?

Popone or Kreuger?
A skipper of the Middle Passage
stinkproof and deaf
with a hundred and seventy slaves
damaged in transit
for Jamaica?

                    Gear and gear.

Shall we consider the evidence in Hatry's case?
Or take Lord Bunting—or
                    UKASE.
          No one to be found outside his own village
                    without
          PAPERS.

     Also, to encourage more efficient tillage,
     2/3 of the produce to be presented to the temporal lord,
     1/5 of the produce to be presented to the parish pope.
          Yours you may say lovingly
                         Boris Godunof.
Or Stalin.

*

Item, the Duke of Slumberwear can get more
by letting the shooting although there is nothing to shoot
but a dozen diseased grouse and a few thin leveret
than by cleaning the ditches to make the ground healthy for sheep.

Lord Cummingway, Lord Tommanjerry, gear and gear,
Lord St Thomas and the Duke of Oppenham
think coals too cheap and costs too dear.

*   *   *   *   *
*   *   *   *   *
*

Gear, then, and gear,
                    gritty-grinding.
The governor spins, raises its arms.
Two three-inch steel cables scream from the drum
seventy fathoms.
We carry lighted Davy lamps,
stoop along narrow track.
Trucks scold tunnel.
In a squat cavern a
naked man on his
knees with a
pickaxe rips a nugget from the coalface.

Four lads
          led the pownies
a mile and a half through rising water,
lampless because the stife
asphyxiates lamps,
by old galleries to the North Shaft.
The water rose.
                    The others
came five months later when it was pumped out
and were buried by public subscription.
(The widows were provided for.)

*

Sing, Ergot and Appiol, didactically:
'Toil! Accumulate Capital!'
Capital is land upon which
work has been done (*vide* textbooks).
Capital is everything except the desert,
sea, untunnelled rock, upper air.
Breathed air
is Capital, though not rented:
70 million tons of solid matter
suspended in the atmosphere,
November, in London,
not by an act of God.

'The sea is his and he
made it'—Who
made Holland and whose is it?

**MAN IS NOT AN END-PRODUCT,
MAGGOT ASSERTS.**

Make? For the making? The system limps.
Everything in this category is deformed,
even the bookkeeping.
Waste accumulates at compound interest.

**MAN IS AN END-PRODUCT AFFIRMS
BLASPHEMOUS BOLSHEVIK.**

UNCOLLECTED ODES

Coryphée gravefooted precise, dance to the gracious music
Thoughts make moving about, dance to the mind's delicate symphony.

2 AGAINST THE TRICKS OF TIME

Why should I discipline myself to verse
Blasting everyday occurrences
With a false flavour of longevity,
Malignantly prolonging
Two corsets in a shop window,
Mumbling indiscreet apologies as now
For what is singularly my own affair,
Or prophesying Death, the kind unmaker
In whom no man has faith? Utterly poet, therefore
Adrift, perusing neglected streets, I
Suppose I ought to be ashamed of myself.

Farewell, ye sequent graces,
Voided faces, still evasive!
Silent be our leave-taking
And mournful

As your night-wanderings
In unlit rooms or where the glow
Of wall-reflected street-lamp-light
The so slow moon

Or hasty matches shadowed large
And crowded out by imps of night
Glimmer on cascades of
Fantom dancers.

Airlapped and silent Muses of light!
Cease to administer
Poisons to dying memories to stir
Pangs of old rapture,

Cease to conspire
Reunions of the inevitable seed
Long blown, barren, sown, gathered
Haphazard to wither.

The dragon rides the middle air like an irresistible wind
Flowing from and to all quarters simultaneously.
His birth is cloudlike of the sea and sun,
Dispersion his life, his death acclaiming voices.
He is the foe, the harbinger. The saints invoke
Michael PROPTER NOS HOMINES ET PROPTER
NOSTRAM SALUTEM but the silent dragon's
Insinuated claw in wincing souls
Answers their supplication. He abets
Indifference with ceaseless splendour
Smudging sketched tables valiantly renewed.
He unsays all words that have passed between men.

3 READING X'S COLLECTED WORKS

I . . .
cemetery of other men's bastards let
wane and peter out
because I am jealous of the Muse's fornications
and over timid to be a cuckold!

Meanwhile you
have raised a sufficient family of versicles;
like you in the main.

4 HYMN TO ALIAS THOR

STRENGTH
inked with a light brush
in the copper kettledrum.

Strength,
the edges turned down.

(Inverted scorpion)
Focus, strength,
focus of percussions.

Sky convenient in conversation, viz.,
for efficiency's sake,
blindness to the street

where a taxidriver
cocks his patentleather cappeak
perpendicularly over a squint at the weather
calculating chances
of reaching rank's head before lunch.

Or, the neatcreased laundryfresh handkerchief
might anticipate a sneeze
(if linen web trembles to thinking's tuning)

at any nose's tauttipped touch,
receive in convulsion of bloom
snot,

lap over and
cherish till desiccated.

Such charges, coupled lightning,
the rainbow signature on each scroll warrants
genuine, beware of imitations!

The soil refuses the lightning!
Desolate air stagnates over that valley,
winds putrefy, silence, the offered storm

limp, dust hangs damp,
thin mud sags in the air,
a deathstink 's over the whole valley,

vinestakes' curtain of leaves droop
mottled blue with wash,
hard peaches, bitter figs,
the stream niggard trickle of gall,

and flies drag sweat over the eyelids
and sour lips.

Thirdly

Oftener the soil accepts the lightning.

5

The flat land lies under water
hedge-chequer-grill above concealing
(not long) heliotrope monotony.

Cold water shin-embracing clacks
desolately, no overtones. Lukewarm
moist socks trickle sea-boot squeezed
black gutters muttering between the toes.
Moreover it rains, drizzles.

Utter-horizon-penetrating glances
spoil only paupers towing derelict home
the flat land hedge-grilled heliotrope under water.

6

Gertie Gitana's hymn to waltzing,
come to think of it, that's the goods.
You, thirdrate muse, Polymnia-alias-Echo,
who'll foster our offspring
begotten in a Waterloo Road three-and-sixpenny
                                    bed-and-breakfast
between indifference and bad habit
established by Erasmus and other idiots
nuts on the classics?
No inclination,
inclination at the wrong time, soul
not at home to callers:
its possibly ultimate inhumation
made flesh under a neat strewing of granite chips
complete with kerb. (But no stone,
Sadi's right, dogs would piss on it.)
Without science, if you please, or psychology!
A mere prescription, as:
'Take one look at the truth about yourself,
you'll never want another.'

'An odds-on favourite's unexciting but
dont back outsiders, its a mugs game',
out of the *selva oscura*, oracle
without authority, 'give over swanking.'

Omar observed: 'Sobriety is unworthy
of anything that has life.' Supplemented
that proposition: 'Turf's pretty till
our grave's turf's pretty.'

Then Barbara
bribing the brain with dud cheques
for any figure on the Bank of Aeolus
(paid up capital twentyone consonants
and five vowels, debtor to
sundry windbags sundry bags of wind,
cent per cent cover in the vaults, vocables
on call or short notice to any amount)
made up so skilfully you wouldnt know her
works the same con-game on the same dupe twice.

Muleteers recite Firdusi, scots sing Burns.
Precedent allows
a moder-rate kettledr-rum r-r-roulade. In practice
keep an eye on the crocodiles, all power
to the congress of murdering crocodiles.
Or check up that syncopated
metre a rising sea never
conforms to?
Double-tongueing a corked flute
descant to the bass:
'Less three per cent deducted for
our compulsory Superannuation Fund.'

O, 'count upon it as a truth next to your creed
that no one person in office of which he is master for life
will ever hazard that office for the good of his country,'
no pedant with established circulation
take Polymnia's hand.
Gertie Gitana's hymn to waltzing
's the goods, you third-rate muse
with your head in the gas oven.

7 ENVOI TO THE READER

From above the moon
    to below the fishes
nobody knows
    my secret heart.
Do you suppose
    I'd publish it?
Spell out a fart
    and have it printed?

8 TRINACRIA

1

Child, I have counted
all the stones in this wall . . .

Even today
to find you alone at home
was impossible.

2

My prospective brother-in-law
sent me a gift, a fan.
It had three different colours,
rose, scarlet and gold.

Everybody asked me:
What did that fan of yours cost you?
I answered: Nothing. My
sister's sweetheart gave it me.

3

On highest summits dawn comes soonest.
(But that is not the time to give over loving.)

4

I went to Hell: never before had I been there!
I did not want to see my sweetheart.

She said to me: Scoundrel and dog!
These pains I undergo on your account.

I said to her: You did not love me,
there are fairer women than you.

9 A SONG FOR RUSTAM

Tears are for what can be mended,
not for a voyage ended
the day the schooner put out.
Short fear and sudden quiet
too deep for a diving thief.
Tears are for easy grief.

My soil is shorn,
forests and corn.
Winter will bare the rock.
What has he left of pride
whose son is dead?
My soil has shaved its head.

The sky withers and stinks.
Star after star sinks
into the west, by you.
Whirling, spokes of the wheel
hoist up a faded day,
its sky wrinkled and grey.

Words slung to the gale
stammer and fail:
'Unseen is not unknown,
unkissed is not unloved,
unheard is not unsung;'
Words late, lost, dumb.

Truth that shone is dim,
lies cripple every limb.
Where you were, you are not.
Silent, heavy air
stifles the heart's leap.
Truth is asleep.

10

To abate what swells
use ice for scalpel.
It melts in its wound
and no one can tell
what the surgeon used.
Clear lymph, no scar,
no swathe from a cheek's bloom.

Such syllables flicker out of grass:
'What beckons goes'; and no glide lasts
nor wings are ever in even beat long.
A male season with paeonies, birds bright under thorn.
Light pelts hard now my sun's low,
it carves my stone as hail mud
till day's net drapes the haugh,
glaze crackled by flung drops.
What use? Elegant hope, fever of tune,
new now, next, in the fall, to be dust.

Wind shakes a blotch of sun,
flatter and tattle willow and oak alike
sly as a trout's shadow on gravel.
Light stots from stone, sets ridge and kerf quick
as shot skims rust from steel. Men of the north
'subject to being beheaded and cannot avoid it
of a race that is naturally given that way'.
'Uber sophiae sugens' in hourless dark,
their midnight shimmers like noon.
They clasp that axle fast.

Those who lie with Loki's daughter,
jawbones laid to her stiff cheek,
hear rocks stir above the goaf;
but a land swaddled in light? Listen, make out
lightfall singing on a wall mottled grey
and the wall growls, tossing light,
prow in tide, boulder in a foss.
A man shrivels in many days, eyes thirst for night
to scour and shammy the sky
thick with dust and breath.

Dentdale conversation

Yan tan tethera pethera pimp
nothing to waste but nothing to skimp.
Lambs and gimmers and wethers and ewes
what do you want with political views?
Keep the glass in your windows clear
where nothing whatever's bitter but beer.

UNCOLLECTED OVERDRAFTS

Night swallowed the sun as
the fish swallowed Jonas.

(Sa'di)

Many well-known people have been packed away in cemeteries,
there is no longer any evidence that they ever existed.
That old corpse they shovelled under the dirt,
his dust's so devoured not a bone of him's left.

Naushervan's honourable name survives because he was
open-handed,
though a lot has happened since Naushervan died.
—Better be open-handed, What's-your-name, (write it off:
Depreciation)
before the gossip goes: 'What's-his-name's dead.'

(Sa'di)

Light of my eyes, there *is* something to be said.
Drink and give to drink while the bottle is full.
Old men speaking from experience, as I told you:
'Indeed, you will grow old.
Love has respectable people chained up for the torture.
You'd like to rumple his hair? Give up being good.
Rosary and veil have no such relish as drink.'

Put it in practice. Send for the wine-merchant.
Amongst the drinkers, one lifetime,
one purse cannot cramp you.
A hundred lives for your dear!
(In love's business the devil lacks not ideas,
but listen, listen with your heart to the angel's message.)

Maple leaves wither, gaiety's not everlasting.
Wail, O harp! Cry out, O drum!
May *your* glass never want wine!
Look gently behind you and drink.
When you step over the drunks in your gold-scattering gown
spare a kiss for *Hafiz* in his flannel shirt.

(Hafiz)

O everlastingly self-deluded!
  If there's no love for you there's nothing for it
but to go crazy. Anyway, dont set up for
  a paragon of self-restraint.
Love's dizziness cant invade a head
  dizzy with alcohol?
You're jaundiced, misery-hideous!
  Anybody can read your symptoms.
Give respectability and pride the go-by, *Hafiz*,
cadge yourself a drop of booze and get
                    crapulously drunk.

(Hafiz)

Isnt it poetical, a chap's mind in the dumps?
Of course our cliché's true:
'Your lips the seal on my passport
that's a hundred empires in hand.'
So, my heart, dont wince when they mock you,
mockeries rightly regarded are riches:
who doesnt take ghoulish sarcasms thus,
his marble was hacked out in haste.
Wine and tears in a cup—each offers it someone;
that's only polite, under Providence:
the routine of the perfumery business,
one rose crushed, one kept.
And it's false, the frenzy quitting *Hafiz*,
the durable frenzy warranted to
                              last ever so long.

(Hafiz)

191

I'm the worse for drink again, it's
got the better of me.
A thousand thanks to the red wine
put colour in my face.
I'll kiss the hand that gathered the grapes.
May he never trudge who trod them out!

You'd dock my drink for the fast, you!
God doesn't trifle.
Born with 'Rake' scrawled
on my forehead, dare you erase it?
Talk about wisdom! When it comes to dying
the soul may struggle—like a doomed hero.

Settle down, no nagging, placidity
's silk next your skin. If you
want eternity do so
they'll never use past tense of you.
Drink as *Hafiz*, you'll gather impetus
world without end.

(Hafiz)

From FARIDUN'S SONS

Faridun watched the road
and the army missed the young king.
When the time came for his homecoming
they were getting a welcome ready,
wine, music and dancers.
They had fetched the drums and led the elephants
out of the stable,
hung the whole land with garlands.
  . . . A cloud of dust on the road,
presently a fast camel,
a rider in mourning, keening,
a gold box on his lap,
in the box a piece of brocade,
in the brocade . . . !
Came to Faridun,
pale, crying, sighing woe,
they could not make out what he said,
prised the lid off the box,
snatched the cloth, there was Iraj's head.
Faridun fell from his horse like a dead man.
The army tore their clothes,
not for this the king
led them out, this return, torn flags,
drums reversed, drawn faces;
kettledrums, elephants foreheads, draped black,
the horses splashed with indigo,
a dismounted general, an army dismounted,
dust on their heads, officers gnawing their arms,
or calling out:
                'Never fancy Fate favours you,
the heavens turning above us
ready to snatch whatever they smile on.
Defy them, they smile. Call them Friend,
they never return your devotion.'

To Iraj's garden,
merry at festival time,
Afaridun with unsteady steps,
clutching the young king's head,

his son's head.
He looked at the gorgeous throne—
tawdry without the king,
and the pool, the cypresses,
rosetrees, willows, quinces.
When they strewed dust on the throne
a wail from the army,
groaning, tearing their hair, shedding tears,
clawing their own cheeks.
Faridun put on the ritual crimson sash,
set the pleasure house alight,
dug up the flowerbeds, burned the cypresses,
all the eye's delight,
and hugging Iraj's head turned to heaven:

'God of justice, see how the innocent fare!
His head, the marks of the knife on the neck, I have it.
His body, devoured.
Scald those cruel hearts, let their days be black, all,
blister their hearts, let their hurts fester
till brute beasts pity them.
You who adjust all things, let me find refuge from Time
till I see one of Iraj's blood make ready for vengeance,
till I see those heads cut off like this innocent head.
Then of your mercy let the soil take my measure.'

He mourned so long on the bare ground
his beard grew down to his chest. Wept his sharp eyes blind,
behind closed doors in the great hall.
'You brave young man, no king ever died as you did,
no king beheaded by devils
wild beasts' maws his coffin.'

There was such crying and keening
even the animals could get no sleep.
Assemblies, every man and woman
throughout the country with tears in their eyes,
in black, past consolation,
many a day, as though all life were death.

(Firdosi)

194

BAUDELAIRE IN CYTHERA

Heart trapezing gaily about the ropes: hull
a-roll under a clear sky.

                        —That sombre beach?
—Songfamous Cythera.

                    —Indeed?

                            —Yes,
bachelor's paradise. Look at it . . . wretched place!
Festivals of love, eh? . . . whispers and all that?

The moist smell of amours clings to it, isle of blown
roses, still adored. Devout whimpers drift
above like pollen, like ringdove murmurs. A harsh
stony hungry land, harassed by shrill cries.
Nothing Baedeker stars: though I did see something . . .

Not a temple shaded by ancient planes, nor yet
a young priestess of love slacking her tunic to
feel the breeze. We ranged very close in shore,
so close our sails set the birds fluttering over a
black gallows cut out of the sky.

                                  They were perched on
carrion, their beaks driven precisely into
putrid sores. The eyes, rotted. Heavy bowels
dangling. Vultures had castrated him. Dogs
were howling.

               Cytherean!
Child of sublime skies! Comic corpse, wretched
contemptible corpse!

Bright sky, shining sea, Venus' land; Baudelaire
bows to Baudelaire through the looking-glass.

(After Baudelaire)

Amru'l Qais and Labīd and Akhtal and blind A'sha and Qais
who keened over the bones of dead encampments and fallen tents,
as we mourn for the ruins of poetry and broken rhymes—
Bu Nuvās and Bu Haddād and Bu Malik bin al Bashar,
Bu Duvaid and Bu Duraid and Ibn Ahmad. Do you hear
him who sang 'She has warned us,' who sang 'The honest sword,'
who sang 'Love has exhausted'—?
Bu'l Ata and Bu'l Abbās and Bu Salaik and Bu'l Mathil,
and the bard of Lavaih and the Harper of Herat.
Where are the wise Afghans, Shuhaid and Rudaki,
and Bu Shakūr of Balkh and Bu'l Fath of Bust likewise.
Bid them come and see our noble century
and read our poetry and despair—

(Manuchehri)

Night is hard by. I am vexed and bothered by sleep.
Dear my girl, bring me something to cure me of sleep.
Not quick and alert, as well be dead as asleep:
what argument have the dead? How shall the sleeping answer?

I for one strive not to die before my time.
Who shall hire the untimely dead? Have they compensation?
I snatch the sleep from my eyes with strong wine,
aye! with strong wine, foe of a young man's sleep.

Much do I wonder at him whom sleep bears away
where there is yet a bottle of wine in the house,
and yet more wonder at him who drinks without music,
without an air on the harp, guzzles his wine.
No horse will drink without you whistle to him:
is a man less than a horse, water more than wine?

Three things, and the more the better, nourish the free:
one is wine and one is music and one is meat.
No cash let there be among us, no book, no dice:
these are three things unfitting to our freedom.
Books to the school, cash to the marketplace,
dice to the taverns of the low.
We, men of wine are we, meat are we, music . . .
Well, then! wine have we, meat have we, music . . .

(Manuchehri)

You, with my enemy, strolling down my street,
you're a nice one! Aren't you ashamed to meet me?
Didn't you call me 'malignant', and 'quarrelsome'?
Don't you complain of my 'impossible' character?

You looked round and found someone more to your liking.
You escaped neatly from my 'temper' and 'dullness'.
Plainly, your love is flooding his brook:
the day is gone when it trickled into mine.

Now that you've found someone such as you wanted
why do you blunder so far down my street?

(Manuchehri)

The thundercloud fills meadows with heavenly beauty,
gardens with plants, embroiders plants with petals,
distils from its own white pearls brilliant dyes,
makes a Tibet of hills where its shadow falls,
San'a of our fields when it passes on to the desert.
Wail of the morning nightingale, scent of the breeze,
frenzy a man's bewildered, drunken heart.
Now is the season lovers shall pant awhile,
now is the day sets hermits athirst for wine.

Shall I sulk because my love has a double heart?
Happy is he whose she is singlehearted!
She has found me a new torment for every instant
and I am, whatever she does, content, content.
If she has bleached my cheek with her love, say: Bleach!
Is not pale saffron prized above poppy red?
If she has stooped my shoulders, say to them: Stoop!
Must not a harp be bent when they string it to sing?
If she has kindled fire in my heart, say: Kindle!
Only the kindled candle sends forth light.
If tears rain from my eyes, say: Let them rain!
Spring rains make fair gardens. And if then
she has cast me into the shadow of exile, say:
Those who seek fortune afar find it the first.

(Manuchehri)

Hi, tent-boy, get that tent down.
The first are gone and one drum's growled,
loads on the camels, nearly prayer-time,
and tonight full moon, up as soon
as the sun drops behind Babyl.

O silver-white Sanubar! Could a day
fade without our noticing?
Leave me now, lovely girl.
There'll be no harvest of the love we sowed.

—Tears pelting as though pepper thrown
had blistered her eyes, stumbling and fluttering
she belted her arms around me,
hung as a sword hangs, crying:
'Is it to please all jealous Primnesses?
How can I tell whether you will come back?
Perfect I thought you in every art,
but in love you are not perfect.'
And I: 'I am no tyro.
Love's taste's sharpest at a hasty parting.'

Patience heavy on my heart, I looked
where the tents had been, and the camels,
saw neither mount nor rider
but my Najib, restless;
loosed the hobbles from her knees
like one releasing a bird from a fowler's net;
made the headstall fast at her ears' root,
slung the blanket loose to her shoulder,
mounted. She leapt to go,
I praying: 'God make it easy',
counting her steps for the stages
as surveyors measure the ground,
into a hard, cold desert.
Wind froze my blood, the pools frozen
like silver dishes on a gold tray.

Before morning night was blacker
for the white snow wasting away
and out of the hard ground rose a mud like fishglue.
One long watch of the night
was done when the Dogstar rose
bright over Mosul's mound,
then the Great Bear, and I came close
behind the caravan like a boat nearing the beach.
The sound of their anklets reached me
with chatter and clatter of bells
and I saw the peacock litters
stilted on herony legs;
bells within bells, gilded,
hanging to the camels' knees,
and lances, making the valley a cornfield.

(After Manuchehri)

You've come! O how flustered and anxious I've been,
chill as a stone ever since you went away
but not forgetful; silent, yes, and confused,
longing, longing always to see you again.

Without you I've not slept, not once, in the garden
nor cared much whether I slept on holly or flock,
lonely to death between one breath and the next
only to meet you, hear you, only to touch;

waiting all night for the breeze to bring me your scent
till the cocks called up the sun from jail, and
poppy, peony, primula glowed yet I
shivered and sank, sick for consolation
sick day long for the pain of your going, saying
'You broke your word. I have stood fast by mine.'

You broke your word. I have stood fast by mine,
counting old kisses, tasting past praise again,
a heavy, cumbersome bundle not to set down;
but 'Keep' you said. I've let no dust of it drop.

Thorns in our tangled garden pock my cheeks
when I go down to the burn, eyes turned in
from day to a night in my head, your night,
heavy for ever over the garden now.

At the heel of my door they'll ask what fruit life bore.
Tell them the night I talked with my darling was sweet.
Who has judged that the bond you gave then is null,
judged unjustly. I have performed my part.
Will you be glad one day to hear me greet you:
'You've come. O how flustered and anxious I've been.'

(After Sa'di)

Ginger, who are you going with?
Some slim kid? One who squeezes you
among the early meadowsweet?
You do your hair to please him,
or he thinks so, loose and smooth.

Change your mind and he'll cry.
He's not reckoned with storms
but fancies your glow is
all for him, always at hand,
always gentle; winds don't veer.

You'll shine on them all, poor brats,
till one of them gets you.
But as for me,
I've wrung my shirt out long since.

(Horace)

Like a fawn you dodge me, Molly,
a lost fawn.
A breath of wind scares her.
Leaves rustle, or a rabbit
stirs, and her heart flutters,
her knees quiver.
But it's me chasing you, Molly,
not a tiger, not to tear you.
Let mother go,
you're old enough for a man.

(Horace)

That filly couldnt carry a rider nor
pull her weight in a plow team. How
could she stand up under a stallion?
All she thinks about is fields or a
brook when it's warm to plodge in.
Prancing round with the colts is her fun. Why
bite green apples? Come October they'll redden.
Then she'll match you: Time will give her the years
it snatches from you. She'll toss her head soon
to challenge a man, the besom, cuter
than Jane who hides or Leslie who lets her blouse
slip from her shining shoulder or even Jimmy.
You cant tell him from a girl if he keeps his mouth shut
with his long, loose hair and unguessable face.

(Horace)

Snow's on the fellside, look! How deep,
our wood's staggering under its weight.
The burns will be tonguetied
while frost lasts.

But we'll thaw out. Logs, logs for the hearth!
and dont spare my good whisky. No water, please.
Forget the weather. Elm and ash
will stop signalling
when this gale drops.

Why reckon? Why forecast? Pocket
whatever today brings
and dont turn up your nose, it's childish,
at making love and dancing.
When you've my bare scalp, if you must, be glum.

Keep your date in the park while light's whispering.
Hunt her out, well wrapped up, hiding and giggling,
and get her bangle for a keepsake.
She wont make much fuss.

(Says Horace, more or less)

Poor soul! Softy, whisperer,
hanger-on, pesterer, sponge!
Where are you off to now?
Pale and stiff and bare-bummed,
It's not much fun in the end.

(Hadrian)

NOTES

NOTES TO COLLECTED POEMS

I have left these notes as they were, with hardly an exception. Notes are a confession of failure, not a palliation of it, still less a reproach to the reader, but may allay some small irritations.

[BB]

VILLON III: The image of two drops of quicksilver running together is from the late E. Nesbit's *Story of the Amulet*. To her I am also indebted for much of the pleasantest reading of my childhood.

ATTIS: Parodies of Lucretius and Cino da Pistoia can do no damage and intend no disrespect.

AUS DEM ZWEITEN REICH III: The great man need not be identified but will, I believe, be recognized by those who knew him.

THE WELL OF LYCOPOLIS: Gibbon mentions its effect in a footnote. The long quotations from Villon and Dante will of course be recognized. Americans may care to be informed that as a native of Paphos Venus was until recently entitled to a British passport. Her quotation from Sophie Tucker will not escape the attention of those who remember the first world war, and need not engage that of those who dont. The remarks of the brass head occur in the no longer sufficiently well-known story of Friar Bacon and Friar Bungay, of which I think Messrs Laurel and Hardy could make use. Some may remember that the only one of the rivers of Paradise to which we have access on earth, namely Zamzam, is reported to be brackish.

THE SPOILS: Let readers who lack Arabic forgive me for explaining that the epigraph, *al anfal li'llah*, is from the Qor'an, sura viii, and means 'The spoils are for God'. I named the sons of Shem at random from the Bible's list.

Some Persian words have no English equivalent. An *aivan* is a high arch backed by a shallow honeycomb half-dome or leading into a mosque. *Chenar*, Platanus orientalis, is grander than its London cousins; *tar*, a stringed instrument used in Persian classical music. *Vafur* signifies the apparatus of opium smoking, pipe, pricker, tongs, brazier, charcoal and the drug, shining like a stick of black sealing wax. The *azan* is the mo'ezzin's call to prayer. You hardly hear its delicate, wavering airs at other times, but an hour before sunrise it has such magic as no other music, unless perhaps the nightingale in lands where nightingales are rare.

Proper names explain themselves and can be found in books of reference. A few are not yet filed. *Hajji Mosavvor*, greatest of modern miniature painters, suffered from paralysis agitans. *Naystani*, a celebrated virtuoso of the nose-flute. *Taj* sings classical odes with authenticity; *Moluk-e Zarrabi* moulds them to her liking. *Shir-e Khoda* begins Teheran's radio day with a canto of the epic. *Sobhi* is the most perfect teller of tales, his own.

Gaiety and daring need no naming to those who remember others like *Flight-lieutenant Idema*.

Abu-Ali is, of course, Ibn Sina—Avicenna.

BRIGGFLATTS: The Northumbrian tongue travel has not taken from me sometimes sounds strange to men used to the koine or to Americans who may not know how much Northumberland differs from the Saxon south of England. Southrons would maul the music of many lines in Briggflatts.

An autobiography, but not a record of fact. The first movement is no more a chronicle than the third. The truth of the poem is of another kind.

No notes are needed. A few may spare diligent readers the pains of research.

Spuggies: little sparrows.

May the flower, as haw is the fruit, of the thorn.

Northumbrians should know Eric *Bloodaxe* but seldom do, because all the school histories are written by or for southrons. Piece his story together from the Anglo-Saxon Chronicle, the Orkneyinga Saga, and Heimskringla, as you fancy.

We have burns in the east, *becks* in the west, but no brooks or creeks.

Oxter: armpit.

Boiled louse: coccus cacti, the cochineal, a parasite on opuntia.

Hillside fiddlers: Pianforini, for instance, or Manini.

Lindisfarne, the Holy Island, where the tracery of the Codex Lindisfarnensis was elaborated.

Saltings: marshy pastures the sea floods at extraordinary springs.

Hastor: a Cockney hero.

The Laughing Stone stands in Tibet. Those who set eyes on it fall into violent laughter which continues till they die. Tibetans are immune, because they have no humour. So the Persian tale relates.

The male salmon after spawning is called a *kelt*.

Gabbro: a volcanic rock.

Aneurin celebrated in the Cymric language the men slain at Catterick by the sons of *Ida*, conquerors of Northumberland.

Skerry: O, come on, you know that one.

Hoy: toss, hurl.

Skillet: an American frying pan; and *girdle*, an English griddle.

Fipple: the soft wood stop forming with part of the hard wood tube the wind passage of a recorder.

Scone: rhyme it with 'on', not, for heaven's sake, 'own'.

Gentles: maggots.

Wilson was less known than *Telfer*, but not less skilful.

Sailors pronounce *Betelgeuse* 'Beetle juice' and so do I. His companion is 'Ridgel', not 'Rhy-ghel'.

Sirius is too young to remember because the light we call by his name left its star only eight years ago; but the light from *Capella*, now in the zenith, set out 45 years ago—as near fifty as makes no difference to a poet.

CHOMEI AT TOYAMA: Kamo-no-Chomei flourished somewhat over a hundred years before Dante. He belonged to the minor nobility of Japan and held various offices in the civil service. He applied for a fat job in a Shinto temple, was turned down, and next day announced his conversion to Buddhism. He wrote critical essays, tales and poems; collected an anthology of poems composed at the moment of conversion by Buddhist proselytes (one suspects irony); and was for a while secretary to the editors of the Imperial Anthology.

He retired from public life to a kind of mixture of hermitage and country cottage at Toyama on Mount Hino and there, when he was getting old, he wrote the Ho-Jo-Ki in prose, of which my poem is in the main a condensation. The careful proportion and balance he keeps, the recurrent motif of the house and some other indications suggest to me that he intended a poem more or less elegiac but had not the time nor possibly energy at his then age to invent what would have been for Japan, an entirely new form, nor to condense his material sufficiently. I have taken advantage of Professor Muccioli's Italian version, together with his learned notes, to try to complete Chomei's work for him. I cannot take his Buddhism solemnly considering the manner of his conversion, the nature of his anthology, and his whole urbane, sceptical and ironical temper. If this annoys anybody I cannot help it.

The earth quaked in the second year of Genryaku, 1185.

FIRST BOOK OF ODES: I have taken my chance to insert a couplet in the First Book of Odes and promote *The Orotava Road* from limbo to its chronological place amongst them, which has obliged me to renumber many.

I:7: The quotation might not be readily identified without a hint. It is from Livy.

I:18: The war and the Forestry Commission have outdated this complaint. *Cowpit* means overturned.

I:20: A presumably exact version of Jengiz Khan's correspondence with Chang Chun exists in Bretschneider's *Mediaeval Researches from Eastern Asiatic Sources*. Others more competent than I may prefer to investigate it in the Si-Yu-Ki of Li Chi Chang, one of Chang Chun's disciples who made the journey with him and recorded the correspondence. Pauthier rendered that work, according to Bretschneider, very imperfectly into French.

I:24: The case was tried in 1917 or 1919, I forget.

I:32: In Samangan Rustam begot Sohrab.

I:33: The cool breeze of a pure, uncomprehending rendering of Handel's best known aria.

I:34: Perhaps it is superfluous to mention Darwin's *Formation of Vegetable Mould*.

I:36: A friend's misunderstanding obliges me to declare that the implausible optics of this poem are not intended as an argument for the existence of God, but only suggest that the result of a successful work of art is more than the sum of its meanings and differs from them in kind.

SECOND BOOK OF ODES:

II:5: *Canvas udders*, motarekeh mal moy, the cooling water bags carried through the desert. *Dynast*, Abdulaziz Ibn Saud, of the tribe Aneiza.

II:9: Whoever has been conned, however briefly, into visiting a 'poets' conference' will need no explanation of this ode.

OVERDRAFTS: It would be gratuitous to assume that a mistranslation is unintentional.

NOTE TO THE PIOUS CAT

You must call him 'Obeyed', like the English word 'obeyed a command', 'obeyed a zaw-kaw-nee'; and save most of your breath for the 'nee'. He wrote this story about six hundred years ago, and Persian children still read it at school, or they used to, twenty years since. Any story that lasts as long as that is worth listening to, I think. Perhaps not everything in it is true, but bits of it are very true indeed.

[BB]
1937–77

EDITOR'S NOTES TO
UNCOLLECTED POEMS

With the exception of a single quatrain whose 'circulation' seems to have been largely oral, I have restricted my notes to the purely bibliographical, adding only such comment as seems necessary to establish context. Some archival sources of texts or variants are given. References to Roger Guedalla, *Basil Bunting: a bibliography of works and criticism*, Norwood, PA, 1973, are given as (Guedalla), with the appropriate item reference. The following conventions for Bunting's collections have been used:

(1930): *Redimiculum Matellarum*, Milan, 1930 (Guedalla A1)
(1935): *Caveat Emptor: poems by Basil Bunting*, unpublished TS dated 1935 in the Beinecke Rare Book and Manuscript Library, Yale
(1950): *Poems 1950*, Galveston, 1950 (Guedalla A2)
(1965): *Loquitur*, London, 1965 (Guedalla A5)
(1968): *Collected Poems*, London, 1968 (Guedalla A9)

THEY SAY ETNA: First published in *Active Anthology*, ed. Ezra Pound, London, 1933 (Guedalla B4). Variant included in (1935). Corrupt variant in (1950); quoted in *Confucius to Cummings: an Anthology of Poetry*, ed. Ezra Pound and Marcella Spann, New York, 1964 (Guedalla B10). Faced with three versions, I have chosen that which seems the most self-contained and complete: in this case, the earliest.

UNCOLLECTED ODES:

1: Published as an epigraph in (1930).

2: Published in (1930), included (untitled) in (1935). A version of the central section became 'Farewell ye sequent graces' (Ode I:2) from (1950) onwards.

3: Published in *Whips and Scorpions: Specimens of Modern Satiric Verse*, ed. Sherard Vines, Glasgow, 1932 (Guedalla B2). Included with variant title in (1935).

4: Included in (1935).

5: Included in (1935).

6: Included in (1935).

7: TS in the Harry Ransom Humanities Research Center, Austin, Texas: part of a group of poems (including sections of Uncollected Ode 6, above, and Overdrafts ('Isn't it poetical . . .')) sent to Louis Zukofsky in 1935. Appended to title in TS: '(It dont apply to you, Louis)'. Other copies exist, e.g. variant in letter to Ezra Pound (summer 1935) in the Beinecke Rare Book and Manuscript Library.

8: Included in (1935), with an author's note: 'Only 2 & 4 are Sicilian: the other two are from North Italy.' Part 3 became Ode I:27 from (1965) onwards.

9: TS in the Poetry/Rare Books Collection, S.U.N.Y. at Buffalo, dated 1952–1964 (the first date added in ink, possibly in another hand). Also TS in the Harry Ransom Humanities Research Center, Austin, Texas. Included in *Basil Bunting: a major British modernist* (Ph.D. thesis, University of Wisconsin) by Barbara E. Lesch, Wisconsin, 1979. Published, with some variant spacing, and dated 7:IX:64, in *Sulfur* No. 14, ed. Clayton Eshleman, Los Angeles, 1985. Rustam, Bunting's first son, died in 1952.

10: TS in the Poetry/Rare Books Collection, S.U.N.Y. at Buffalo, dated 1971. Published in *Epitaphs for Lorine*, ed. Jonathan Williams, Champaign, 1973. Lorine Niedecker died in 1970.

11: Some copies typeset and printed by Bunting and circulated to friends c.1972 (e.g. in Mountjoy Collection, Basil Bunting Poetry Archive, Durham University Library). Reprinted in *Music and meaning in the poetry of Basil Bunting* (Ph.D. thesis, University of Notre Dame, Ind.) by Sister Victoria Forde, Notre Dame, 1972. A quotation mark in line 16 has been supplied from MS material in the Mountjoy Collection.

12: Dated 1978. Published in *Truck*, vol. 21, ed. David Wilk, Carrboro, 1979.

UNCOLLECTED OVERDRAFTS:

'Night swallowed the sun . . .': Published in *A Test of Poetry*, ed. Louis Zukofsky, New York, 1948 (Guedalla B6). Version of Sa'di's *Gulistan*, I, iv. Dated by Zukofsky as 'c.1935'. The couplet appears as part of a TS entitled 'The Rosegarden, part one: The Habits of Kings. Tale number four' in the Harry Ransom Humanities Research Center, Austin, Texas. This piece is punctuated by verse fragments, including the following:

> Noah's son took to low company:
>   him prophecy ceased to illumine.
> The dog of the Seven Sleepers became,
>   by prolonged good company, human.

'I am very fond of Noah's son and always recite it whenever there's an opportunity' he added at the foot of the TS. He would still recite it on occasions towards the end of his life.

'Many well-known people . . .': Included in (1935). Version of Sa'di's *Gulistan*, I, ii.

'Light of my eyes . . .': Published in *Bozart-Westminster* vol. 1 (i), ed. T. Jacobs and E. Hartsock, Oglethorpe, 1935 (Guedalla D10). Included (with variants) in (1935). Version of Diwan-i Hafiz (see e.g. H.S. Jarrett's ed., Calcutta, 1881, No. 444).

'O everlastingly self-deluded!': Included in (1935). Version of Hafiz (op. cit., No. 503).

'Isnt it poetical . . .': Included in (1935), also variant TS in the Harry Ransom Humanities Research Center, Austin, Texas (see note on Uncollected Ode 7, above). Version of Hafiz (op. cit., No. 226).

'I'm the worse for drink . . .': Included in (1935), also variant TS in the Harry Ransom Humanities Research Center, Austin, Texas. Version of Hafiz (op. cit., No. 225).

From *Faridun's Sons*: Published in *The Criterion*, vol. 15, ed. T.S. Eliot, London, 1936 (Guedalla D11). A rough version exists as section 7 of a TS headed (in ink) 'About 1/3 of the story of Faridun's Sons' in the Harry Ransom Humanities Research Center, Austin, Texas, together with related Firdosi material in draft form. Version of Firdosi's *Shahnameh*, 'Faridun', ll. 543–92 (see e.g. Tehran, 1934).

Baudelaire in Cythera: Included in (1935). Version based on Baudelaire, *Un Voyage à Cythère*.

'Amru'l Qais and Labīd and Akhtal . . .': Fragment from a MS letter to Zukofsky dated May Day 1939. Included in *Music and meaning in the poetry of Basil Bunting* (Ph.D. thesis, University of Notre Dame, Ind.) by Sister Victoria Forde, Notre Dame, 1972; reprinted in *Basil Bunting: Man and Poet*, ed. Carroll F. Terrell, Orono, 1981. Version of Manuchehri (see e.g. A. Kazimirski's ed., Paris, 1886, No. 87, ll. 9–21).

'Night is hard by . . .': Published in *Nine*, No. 4 (vol. 2 (iii)), ed. Peter Russell, London, 1950 (Guedalla D14). Version of Manuchehri (op. cit., No. 6).

'You, with my enemy . . .': Published (in an earlier form) in *Nine*, No. 11 (vol. 4 (ii)), ed. Peter Russell, London, 1956 (Guedalla D18). Published thus in *Agenda*, vol. 16(i), ed. William Cookson, London, 1978, where it is dated 1949. Also MS, with slight variations, in the Basil Bunting Poetry Archive, Durham University Library (Mountjoy Collection) dated 1949. Version of Manuchehri (op. cit., No. 91).

'The thundercloud fills meadows . . .': Published in *Nine*, No. 11 (vol. 4 (ii)), ed. Peter Russell, London, 1956 (Guedalla, D18). The second section, dated 1949, appears as an Overdraft on its own from (1965) onwards. Version of Manuchehri (op. cit., No. 14, ll. 1–12).

'Hi, tent-boy . . .': TS with MS alterations, dated 1949, in Basil Bunting Poetry Archive, Durham University Library (Mountjoy Collection). Version of Manuchehri (op. cit., No. 29, ll. 1–46).

'You've come! . . .': TS with MS alterations, dated 1974, in Basil Bunting Poetry Archive, Durham University Library (Mountjoy Collection).

'Ginger, who are you going with?': TS with MS alterations, dated 1969, in Basil Bunting Poetry Archive, Durham University Library (Mountjoy Collection). Version of Horace: Odes, I (v).

'Like a fawn you dodge me, Molly': TS with MS alteration, undated, in Basil Bunting Poetry Archive, Durham University Library (Mountjoy Collection). Version of Horace: Odes, I (xxiii).

'That filly couldnt carry a rider . . .': TS, undated, in Basil Bunting Poetry Archive, Durham University Library (Mountjoy Collection). Version of Horace: Odes, II (v).

'Snow's on the fellside, look! . . .': MS in Basil Bunting Poetry Archive, Durham University Library, dated 1977. Published (with variant punctuation) in *Agenda*, vol. 16 (i), ed. William Cookson, London, 1978. Version of Horace: Odes, I (ix).

'Poor soul! . . .': Quoted in *Six Plaints and a Lament for Basil Bunting* by Peter Quartermain, published in *Conjunctions*, vol. 8, ed. Bradford Morrow, New York, 1985. Intended as an ending for an uncompleted longer poem of which Ode II:12 was at one stage an opening (I am grateful to Peter Quartermain for this information). Version of Hadrian (see e.g. Loeb Classical Library vol. 284: *Minor Latin Poets*, 1934).

APPENDICES

Appendix 1: School Poems

In 1916 Bunting published two poems: they are all that remains of his juvenilia (we have no reason to believe that it was ever extensive) and are noteworthy for that reason alone. In recording them here, in appendix form, I make no apology for their immaturity—the earliest poem in *Collected Poems* is still eight years away. Some notes are needed to supply context.

'The Song of the Ackworth Clock' (by Basil C. Bunting, leaver July 1916) appeared in the Annual Report of the Headmaster of Ackworth School for 1916. In the same year Bunting had delivered a prize-winning paper on Whitman which had won the attention of Edward Carpenter: it is hard to identify such progressive tastes with authorship of this almost militantly conventional school poem. Is it just possible to hear cadences which foreshadow the later, more subtle, concern for sound and quantity? Occasionally, certainly, there are perceptible rhythmic echoes of the Buntings' old family friend, the Newcastle pitman poet, Joseph Skipsey.

THE SONG OF THE ACKWORTH CLOCK

Clock beneath the Cupola,
Never near yet never far
   From the Green below!
You have seen a score of years
Full of schoolboy ink and tears,
Cricket's, football's hopes and fears.
   Tell me what you know!
Tick tock, tick tock, tick tock, slow.

When the Lamb goes twirling round
And the classroom windows sound
   With the winds that blow;
No one then upon the scene
Where the footer match has been;
All deserted is the Green.
   Is this what you know?
Tick tock, tick tock, tick tock, slow.

When the Flags are frozen white
With half a foot of sheer delight
    Crisp and even snow;
Sledges running all day long,
All is right and nothing's wrong,
Bursts of happy schoolboy song,
    Is this what you know?
Tick tock, tick tock, tick tock, slow.

When the asphalt bubbles tar,
And lazy lads from near and far
    Wander to and fro,
Or seek the Elms' welcome shade
Where record cricket scores are made,
And Simpson's do a roaring trade.
    Is this what you know?
Tick tock, tick tock, tick tock, slow.

Or when at Easter's happy time
Old Scholars here from every clime
    Make a lordly show:
When Tommy B. meets Johnny A.,
When aged fogeys leap and play,
When all the world feels young and gay.
    Is this what you know?
        Aye, this is what I know;
Tick tock, tick tock, all of this I know,
Tick tock, tick tock, tick tock, slow.

Bunting attended Leighton Park School from September 1916 to 1918.
'Keep Troth' was published in *The Leightonian* in December 1916, over the
name of B.C. Bunting. It may be assumed that every school magazine of
this period (and many of other periods) had their imitations of Henry
Newbolt, and this piece is not a remarkable departure from genre
(though Bunting readers may recognize an enduring trait of voice in 'Be
straight . . . speak true'). The poem is in no way militaristic. Its orthodoxy
is surprising, however, not only in terms of Bunting's other tastes at the
time (he had progressed from Whitman, and was to present papers on
Blake and Kerensky in the coming year), but in the context of his stormy
school career at this stage. Since arriving in September he had repeatedly
expressed his unhappiness at the school, and in October he had laid a
remarkable document before Charles Evans, his headmaster:

'I have utterly failed to be happy here . . . I think there must be
some great underlying difference between North & South which

makes people with Northern manners comfortable & easy to deal with, but people with the Southern manners are, for me, utterly "impossible" & hateful . . . I think it is your duty to give me my fare to Newcastle . . .'

'Keep Troth', in which Quaker reliance upon inner truth triumphs over worldly conflict, may have its origins in the stern-but-fair talking-to which headmaster Evans gave him on this occasion. *The Leightonian* for December 1918, recording with equal pride the doings of soldiers and conscientious objectors, supplies a relevant instance of B.C. Bunting's keeping truth, speaking true: 'B.C. Bunting is serving a sentence of 112 days at Wormwood Scrubbs, after refusing agricultural work on the ground that in effect that was sending another man to fight for him.'

KEEP TROTH

When Algebra is done, boys,
　And Latin is no more;
And when the war is won, boys,—
　When boyhood's past and o'er—
　　What will you do for England,
　　　Who's done so much for you?
　　Keep troth, speak true, for England,
　　　Be straight, keep troth, speak true.

And while we're still at school, boys,
　The principle's the same;
Stick to the golden rule, boys,
　Play up, and play the game.
　　What do you do for England,
　　　Who does so much for you?
　　Keep troth, speak true for England,
　　　Be straight, keep troth, speak true.

And when you're growing old, boys,
　And sinking to your grave,
You'll find that it will nerve you,
　The rule the Captain gave,—
　　What have you done for England?
　　　How will you answer, you?
　　I've lived a Man for England,
　　　Kept troth, and spoken true.

Appendix 2: Limericks

Bunting's enthusiasm for all forms of 'folk poetry'—including the limerick—is well known, and several pieces have been brought to my attention as potentially having been written by him. In most cases, authentication is practically impossible. The two limericks which follow were however both published over Bunting's name, with his permission, in his lifetime. The first is from a letter from Bunting to Ezra Pound, early in 1935, where he notes 'my limerick . . . got itself collected some years ago & privately printed in Wien . . .' (this edition remains untraced). It was reprinted in *Truck*, vol. 21, ed. D. Wilk, Carrboro, 1979. The second was published in *62 Climerikews to amuse Mr. Lear*, ed. Jonathan Williams, DBA/JCA Editions, Denver, 1983. The search for a third, which has reputedly passed into the koine, remains unsuccessful.

The texts require no further note or apology.

1.

What a pity that Bela Bartok
Cannot give his smug public a shock
    By writing in parts
    For the hiccups and farts
And conducting the piece with

2.

That volatile poet called Jonathan
He never gets here till he's gone again.
He holds one night stands
In a great many lands
But folks think he's just making fun o'them.

INDEX OF TITLES AND FIRST LINES

224

OXFORD POETS

Fleur Adcock

Moniza Alvi

Joseph Brodsky

Basil Bunting

Tessa Rose Chester

Daniela Crašnaru

W. H. Davies

Michael Donaghy

Keith Douglas

D. J. Enright

Roy Fisher

Ida Affleck Graves

Ivor Gurney

David Harsent

Gwen Harwood

Anthony Hecht

Zbigniew Herbert

Tobias Hill

Thomas Kinsella

Brad Leithauser

Derek Mahon

Jamie McKendrick

Sean O'Brien

Alice Oswald

Peter Porter

Craig Raine

Zsuzsa Rakovszky

Henry Reed

Christopher Reid

Stephen Romer

Carole Satyamurti

Peter Scupham

Jo Shapcott

Penelope Shuttle

Anne Stevenson

George Szirtes

Grete Tartler

Edward Thomas

Charles Tomlinson

Marina Tsvetaeva

Chris Wallace-Crabbe

Hugo Williams